P9-DWJ-375

Hints for a
Healthy Planet

A Perigee Book

Perigee Books
are published by
The Putnam Publishing Group
200 Madison Avenue
New York, NY 10016

Copyright © 1990 by King Features Syndicate, Inc.
All rights reserved. This book, or parts thereof, may not be reproduced in any
form without permission. Published simultaneously in Canada
Illustrations copyright © 1990 by Lisa Amoroso.

Library of Congress Cataloging-in-Publication Data

Heloise.
    Heloise, hints for a healthy planet.
        p.   cm.
    ISBN 0–399–51625–5
    1. Environmental protection—Citizen participation—Miscellanea.
I. Title.   II. Title: Hints for a healthy planet.
TD170.2.H44   1990   89–72112 CIP
363.7′057—dc20

Printed in the United States of America
1 2 3 4 5 6 7 8 9 10

This book has been printed on acid-free paper.

∞

My very warm thanks to Eugene Brissie, my favorite publisher, who suggested putting all these classic Heloise hints on recycling and conserving together. My ever faithful and cheerful Marcy Meffert, researcher and friend, who helps make my work load tolerable, and Sandy Brown for digging through thirty years of hints. And, as always, my sweet, humorous husband, David, who never complains about deadlines or work but always says, "How can I help?"

To our loyal Heloise fans who have always reused, recycled, and conserved to save our precious planet. We only have one mother earth and she deserves our attention.

Hints for a
Healthy Planet

Contents

Introduction

Before I write anything else, I have to tell you that this book is printed on recycled paper. My publisher and I decided to practice what we preach about keeping our planet healthy. Heloise columns have always emphasized the "Three R's"—Recycle, Reuse, and be Resourceful. Many Heloise readers are experts in these "Three R's" because they've practiced them for years.

We all know people who have been considered a bit eccentric by the "disposables" generation because they washed and reused plastic bags and containers, made quilts from old clothing, lap robes from old quilts, pillow cases from sheets, washcloths from towels, saved string and gift-wrap, refused to use "modern" chemicals in their gardens, used simple soaps and kitchen products in their homes, and in general never threw anything out that could still be used somehow for something.

As our landfills fill up with disposables, our beaches are polluted by sewage and medical waste, and our drinking water supplies are threatened by chemical runoff, we are having to admit that these people—the savers—were not so eccentric after all. And their reasons for recycling—thrift and general principles (don't throw it out until it's worn out)—were not eccentric either. We are beginning to realize that thrifty habits such as reusing packaging materials, jars, and other food containers, or not using disposables can make a difference if enough of us become environmentally aware.

A 1988 study conducted for the U.S. Environmental Protection Agency (EPA) revealed that we in the United States produce approximately 157.7 million tons of municipal solid waste—trash—each year. This figure breaks down to about 3.5 pounds of trash produced daily by each American man, woman, and child. The total amount of waste produced each year is expected to grow to 192.7 million tons by the year 2000, as the population increases from the present 240 million people.

A study of 800 household refuse pickups in Phoenix, Arizona, reported in *Good Housekeeping* magazine in September 1989, revealed that a typical suburban family of three generates about 40 pounds of garbage weekly. This amount in rounded percentages included:

Polystyrene foam meat trays, cups, egg cartons, and packaging, 3%

Aluminum, 1%

Disposable diapers, 3%

Wood, textiles such as household repair debris, and old clothing, 5%

Metals such as food cans and nails, 5%

Plastic such as soda bottles and bags, 5%

Glass, 8%

Miscellaneous items made from several materials, 10%

Food, 11%

Paper such as newspapers, boxes, mail, and magazines, 21%

Yard wastes and grass clippings, 23%.

How frightening! How does this compare with your household? Which category of waste could you recycle for reuse? If you put food wastes, paper, yard wastes, and grass clippings into a compost heap to be used as mulch and organic fertilizer in your yard, about 55% of your trash output will be reduced with just one change in your habits. The bonus here is that you also have free and safe soil enrichment!

We Americans generate more than two times the amount of trash per capita that is generated by people in Japan or Europe. Our trash output from 1960 to 1986 grew from 87.5 million tons to 157.7 million tons annually, an 80% increase! A September 5, 1988, *Time* magazine story reported that according to calculations in California, the average citizen there throws away 2,555 pounds of trash annually, and in Los Angeles County, environmentalists estimate that enough trash is generated daily to fill Dodger Stadium with garbage about every nine days! (It should be noted that Los Angeles County, like many other counties across the United States, has become environmentally aware and, like them, has put a priority on plastics control. Nonbiodegradable plastic is a target now that we know how long it lasts. For example, the plastic-foam beverage cups that keep coffee warm for five minutes are likely to last a millennium littered on our roadsides and shorelines or buried in our landfills! It's estimated that hard plastic packaging takes up 30% of municipal landfill space.)

Here are some more numbers to ponder from Recycle America, an Illinois waste management company: Each year Americans dispose of 50 million tons of paper, 2.5 billion tons of glass, 24 million tons of yard waste, 400,000 tons of lead-acid batteries, and 240 million tires.

Yet these materials, if recycled, can be reprocessed to produce many useful products and cut down on consumption of our natural resources: Paper can be recycled and used for cereal boxes, wallboard, cardboard, tissue, and newsprint; aluminum cans can be made into more aluminum cans and lawn furniture, and steel cans into steel for manufacturing or tin; glass becomes new bottles, jars, or fiberglass. Plastics can be recycled into toys; traffic cones; carpet backing; or fiberfill for pillows, jackets, or sleeping bags. Yard wastes can be recycled into topsoil, ground covering, and compost. Lead batteries can be recycled into new batteries, and tires into asphalt, playground mats, and railroad crossings.

Opinions on how much of our trash can be recycled vary from 25% to 80%. Most agree that realistically, recycling can reduce the amount of garbage to be disposed of by 25% over time, with the percentage varying from city to city. Today, only 11% of U.S. cities' solid waste is recycled; 13% is used in waste-to-energy programs; and 76% goes into our landfills, according to Keep America Beautiful, Inc. The EPA has set a goal of recycling 25% of U.S. garbage by 1992, as opposed to the 10% to 11% recycled in the 1980s.

The bad news is that about 80% of U.S. trash is currently buried in landfills, and the U.S. Conference of Mayors has predicted that more than half of this country's 9,300 landfills will face closure in 10 years. Some major cities, such as Philadelphia, are already out of space, and others, such as New York and Los Angeles, will exhaust their landfills in a few years. New York City alone produces 25,000 tons of waste each day!

Some sources say that more than 60% of our landfills have closed in the last 10 years and that more than 40% of the landfills that remain are operating without proper permits and could be closed at any time because they don't meet federal or state standards for human health and environmental protection. Finding new landfills is difficult—everybody needs them, but "not in my neighborhood."

To complicate the trash issue, solutions sometimes become problems. A booklet called *Who's Responsible for the Mess,* published by Dow Plastics, notes that the need for proper disposal of solid waste is one of the dilemmas created by the many benefits of our modern lifestyles and the need to protect public health. Paper cups were invented by a doctor who saw a child drinking from a community water source also used by people infected with tuberculosis.

Paper cups prevent spread of infection but need disposal. When we disposed of our garbage in dumps, we found that the rats attracted to dumps carried diseases, so we started burning our garbage. When we found that the smoke and air pollution from burning garbage were unacceptable, we buried it. Then we found out that buried garbage polluted our drinking water.

Putting garbage in plastic bags has become a sanitary and convenient means of disposing of it. When we learned that plastic bags could last for centuries, research resulted in biodegradable and photodegradable bags. But as this book is being written, our scientific and environmental communities are involved in a controversy over biodegradable trash bags. Some experts are saying that while people feel good about using them, degradability is only a marketing tool. "Photodegradable" bags, which are treated with a chemical resin that makes them break down in sunlight, don't break down when they are buried in landfills. "Biodegradable" bags, which are supposed to break down underground, probably won't in today's air- and watertight landfills. In either case, some experts are saying, the plastic never really goes away. It just breaks down into smaller pieces so that what is left behind is a plastic dust, containing certain toxic additives, which is more dangerous than a plastic bag littering the highway. Still others are warning that publicity over photodegradable bags will cause some people to toss their bagged garbage along the highway because they assume the sun will take care of disposal.

Sometimes we can't practice conservation. For example, when the state maximum security prison in Somers, Connecticut, planned to replace disposable plastic spoons and forks with metal ones to save money and benefit glutted landfills, prison guards were outraged; they feared that prisoners would make weapons from the metal utensils (*USA Today,* October 9, 1989).

Time magazine's September 5, 1988, issue reported that

incinerators can reduce garbage weight by 70% while producing heat for generating electricity and that new technology in building incinerators can help remove many pollutants from the environment. However, some environmentalists say that incinerators synthesize dioxin, a very poisonous substance. They say that this problem isn't solved by using scrubbers and other filters that take dioxin from smoke because the dioxin still remains in concentrated form in the ash residue, which then becomes a hazardous waste, which in turn is difficult to dispose of safely.

Obviously, we don't have all the answers to our environmental questions. But that's no reason to give up. Each of us can do something while science wrestles with the solutions to environmental problems—and we can do it now, with today's knowledge.

We can conserve our natural resources by using less energy and water. We can concern ourselves with the chemicals that we and industry put into the environment. We can cut our trash output by one-third to one-half simply by trying to use everything that comes into our homes more than one time, whether it's a paper towel or the packages and containers that come with products we buy. We can use mild and environmentally safe cleaning solutions in our homes. We can use alternatives to harmful chemicals in our yards and still grow green lawns and productive gardens.

Some people are afraid that environmentally safe and biodegradable containers make consumer prices go up and that people won't bother to recycle, but manufacturers are proving otherwise. In its booklet *Questions and Answers About Solid Waste,* Procter & Gamble points out that using the minimum packaging needed to protect the product, to allow it to be used conveniently, and to carry the printed information required by law or for proper use helps to hold down costs and prices of products.

There is other good news. *Changing Times* magazine reports that in the last four years, the volume of recycled plastic soda bottles has doubled, to 150 million pounds, and that of recycled milk jugs has gone from zero to 70 million pounds. The plastics industry says this is only 20% of all the bottles that could be recycled; the goal by mid-1990 is to recycle 50% of soda bottles. A pilot plant run by Mobil and Genpak in Leominster, Massachusetts, can take three million pounds of school-cafeteria polystyrene each year (about the amount used by 1,000 schools) and turn it into recycled foam for insulation, flowerpots, and other packaging. A code on container bottoms helps to speed up sorting; it identifies the material as PET (polyethylene terephthalate) or HDPE (high-density polyethylene).

The best news is that voluntary community recycling programs are working in many parts of the country. In my neighboring city of Austin, Texas, for example, 110,000 of 160,000 homes participate in a voluntary recycling program in which families separate their garbage for recycling: bottles and cans in one sack, newspapers in another, everything else into a third container. It's the first program of its kind in Texas. Where I live, in San Antonio, Texas, the interest in recycling is growing, with most drives being held for newspapers and aluminum collection.

More good news was reported by syndicated Washington Post Writers Group columnist Neil Pierce in July 1989. He wrote that in March 1989, the city of Minneapolis ruled that by July 1990, all food and beverage packaging must be "environmentally acceptable"—recyclable, returnable, or degradable. Its neighboring city, St. Paul, in the same month ruled that plastic-foam egg cartons, plastic ketchup or peanut butter jars, and plastic grocery bags, cups, trays, and plates will all be illegal. In May 1989, Nebraska legislators outlawed the sale of nondegradable disposable diapers in 1993, and similar laws are being discussed in Oregon, Iowa, and Washington. Eighty percent of diapers sold in the United States are disposable ones, which we now know take more than 200 years to decompose.

On July 14, 1989, New York City began a mandatory program that aims to achieve 25% recycling of its waste over the next five years. Rhode Island provides special recycling bins for its residents. If the bin isn't on the curb, the unseparated trash is left behind. New Jersey has made it illegal to dump leaves in landfills. And Washington, D.C., where paper accounts for 50% of the waste, passed a bill requiring 45% of all paper to be recycled by 1994.

Some cities have turned recycling into very positive community experiences. For example, Wellesley, Massachusetts (about 25 miles from downtown Boston, with a population of 27,000), has developed a voluntary dropoff recycling center and disposal facility, where residents bring separated garbage (recyclables) and unseparated garbage. About 83% of residents participate. Dropoff boxes there are clearly marked for glass, newspaper, corrugated cardboard, mixed paper, tin cans, aluminum, batteries, nonferrous and ferrous metal, used oil, plastic bottles, yard waste, firewood, and tires. There is also a reusable items corner for the exchange of books, games, toys, appliances, furniture, and clothes, as well as an area for composting leaves, grass, and other yard wastes.

What makes this program unique is that the dropoff center is also a community park and social gathering center. Picnic tables, well-maintained lawns, trees, flowers, and a circular drive make the site popular for political gatherings and other community benefit events such as Girl Scout cookie sales.

In 1988, recycling rose to 24% of the town's residential trash, and the benefits affected "the bottom line" as well as the environment. The town's net benefit was about $186,000 from sales of recyclables and avoided hauling and landfill costs.

On our coastlines, beach pollution and its effect upon business "bottom lines" is making allies out of environmentalists and the resort industry, two groups that are often at odds over development of beachfront property and coastal wetlands. In the summer of 1989, at least 80 beaches in New York and New Jersey alone were temporarily closed because of garbage or sewage. Pollution is bad business and bad for business—that's what the American Resort and Residential Development Association in Washington, D.C., says.

But perhaps the best reason given by more and more people and businesses for being nice to nature and preserving our world for future generations is the ethical reason. Spokespersons for Procter & Gamble, which is conducting several ecology projects, such as using recycled plastic containers, using recycled cardboard for cartons, and reducing the volume of Pampers diapers, say that "it's the right thing to do" (*USA Today,* August 23, 1989). The Environmental Defense Fund, an organization linking the scientific, economic, and legal communities, and the Advertising Council, an agency that conducts public service campaigns, have come up with a slogan to encourage recycling of solid waste in this country: "If you're not recycling, you're throwing it all away."

After generations of using, and, unfortunately, in some cases abusing, our environment, we've learned that we must be nicer to nature. Whether you call it "the green tide," "going for the green," or "heightened awareness of our precious environment," the time to get on the healthy planet bandwagon is now, because it is "the right thing to do." Some ecologists say that in the twenty-first century, recycling up to 95% of our waste may become standard procedure; if that happens, leaky landfills polluting our water supplies will disappear, ocean dumping will be history, our beaches will be clean, and our planet will be healthy.

I hope this book and the hints in it will be just the beginning for all who read it. We mustn't look upon changing our disposable ways and environmentally unsound practices as a burden. Instead, we need to think of saving the environment for the future as a challenge in which we can develop our best resourceful, innovative, and creative ideas and then share them with others as I have shared the ideas in this book.

Also, I don't think most of us want to totally give up the

convenience of using disposable paper plates, cups, diapers, and so forth. And I doubt that we will recycle every single thing that comes into the house by using all of the hints in this book, which offers, for example, about 60 ways to reuse old panty hose, at least 25 uses for 35mm film canisters, and more than 119 (Actually, we lost count!) uses for plastic containers and packaging.

We have to be realistic. Most of us are so accustomed to modern conveniences that we just can't give them up entirely; we can, however, use them more wisely and with an environmental consciousness. For example, use the same paper cup all day when you're at your vacation cottage; when you're at home, use paper towels more than once—wipe your hands and then use that towel to absorb grease from a frying pan; use disposable diapers only when you travel, and so on. Stop using disposable products, and if there is a certain disposable, such as diapers or paper towels, that you just can't give up, try to be more conserving in other ways. We're all in this environmental challenge together and each of us has to do something for the good of all.

If you have any hints for a healthy planet to share, you can send them to me: Heloise, P.O. Box 795000, San Antonio, TX 78279. Or FAX it: 1-512-HELOISE.

RECYCLING DICTIONARY

Many new buzzwords and terms are used in connection with the concepts and technology of ecology, and you'll be seeing more and more of them on product labels in the supermarkets. I'm listing a few for you, drawn from information provided by Keep America Beautiful, Inc., a national nonprofit, public education organization dedicated to improving waste handling practices in American communities. You will find information from this group's booklet, *Over-*

view: Solid Waste Disposal Alternatives, throughout this book.

◆ *Biodegradable Material:* Waste material that can be broken down, usually by bacteria, into basic elements. Most organic wastes (food, paper, etc.) are biodegradable.

◆ *Composting:* Controlled decomposition of organic solid waste in the presence of oxygen, whereby waste materials become soil additives such as humus or mulch.

◆ *Integrated Solid Waste Management:* A practice of disposing solid waste by such means as reduction, recycling, composting, waste-to-energy, and landfill.

◆ *Leachate:* A liquid that results from rain flowing through landfills containing water, decomposed waste, and bacteria. Unless it is collected and treated in "sanitary" landfills, it can contaminate water supplies.

◆ *Municipal Solid Waste (MSW):* Nonhazardous waste from homes, business, and industry. MSW does not include sewage sludge or industrial, agricultural, or mining wastes.

◆ *Photodegradable:* A process in which the sun's ultraviolet radiation destroys plastic's strength and ability to flex and stretch, causing it to fragment into smaller pieces. Photodegradable plastics disintegrate into plastic dust. Plastics: Three types of plastic are being successfully recycled at this time, and research continues on others. Plastics make up about 7% of municipal solid waste by weight (about 20% by volume) and are expected to be 20% by 2000.

1. *PET* (Polyethylene terephthalate) is most commonly used for soft-drink containers; it can be recycled for use in nonfood products such as carpet backing, fiberfill for sleeping bags, rigid urethane form insulation, fiberglass bathtubs, and various automotive parts.

2. *HDPE* (High-density polyethylene), commonly used for milk jugs and base cups of PET soft-drink bottles, can also be recycled for use in nonfood products such as new base cups for soft-drink containers, trash cans, and "plastic lumber" for railroad ties, decking, and fencing. It's better than wood for many purposes because it doesn't rot and needs no painting—the color can be pigmented into the material.

3. *Polystyrene foam* (Styrofoam) items such as cups, plates, and fast-food carryout containers can be collected, cleaned, and converted into pellets to be combined with other plastic materials to produce plastic lumber for walkways and benches or building insulation and packaging materials.

    Plastics that cannot be separated because they are found in containers made from a variety of resins can be recycled to produce dense materials for fenceposts or park benches. Plastic bags of low-density polyethylene can also be recycled.

◆ *Recycling:* Separation, collection, and processing of waste or secondary products for use in the manufacture of the same or another product (e.g., ground glass can be made into new glass or into fiberglass).

◆ *Resource Recovery:* Extracting and using waste products for use as secondary materials in the manufacture of new products or for conversion to fuel or energy.

◆ *Sanitary Landfill:* Land where refuse is deposited without causing hazards to public health or safety. Fill areas are prepared to control water drainage and to confine the refuse to the smallest possible volume. After the area is filled with refuse, it is covered and reclaimed for recreational use such as conversion to parks or golf courses. Sanitary landfills have systems to collect leachate, control methane gas, and monitor other environmental indicators.

♦ *Scrap Tires:* More than a billion tires are discarded each year, and many states ban them from landfills. This stockpile of tires can be reused in various ways.

1. *Reclaimed rubber* is a process in which tires are shredded and pulverized and formed into sheet rubber for manufacturing molded materials and semi-pneumatic tires.
2. *Retreading* requires about 30% of the energy needed to produce new tires and provides nearly 80% of the mileage of a new tire.
3. *Artificial reefs* can be created when old tires are strung together with noncorrosive cable and holes are drilled in them so they sink in the water.
4. *Refuse-derived fuel systems* may incinerate tires. Some waste-to-energy plants burn only chipped tires and other plants burn whole tires to produce electricity.
5. *Crumb rubber* is ground, shredded rubber that is added to other materials to manufacture new products, including asphalt-rubber and other rubber or plastic products.

♦ *Solid Waste Management:* Systematic collection, source separation, storage, transportation, transfer, processing, treatment, and disposal of solid waste.

♦ *Source Separation:* Separating various waste materials at the point of origin, such as the household, where families separate paper, metal, and glass from the rest of their garbage.

♦ *Source Reduction:* Reducing the amount of waste generated. Manufacturers and consumers are taking an active role in source reduction by buying fewer disposable products, using less packaging or packaging made from recycled materials, decreasing the toxic substances in products, and extending products' useful life. The EPA has called for a 25%

reduction in waste through source reduction activities and recycling by 1992.

♦ *Waste-to-Energy Incineration:* System in which municipal solid waste is burned as received or after being processed, to produce steam or electricity. Waste-to-energy plants can decrease garbage volume by 60% to 90% while recovering energy from discarded products. More than 100 are operating in the United States.

Inside the House

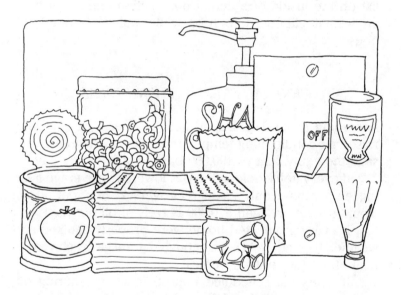

Your home is the place where you make the rules, and so it's the best place for you to start conserving our natural resources and changing the amount of trash produced by your home activities.

Try to make "going green" a challenging game for your family or a personal challenge if you live alone. Everybody wins the "green" game because the prize is a cleaner environment for all of us. The bonus is that "going green" means more than saving resources; it saves other "green" (money), too.

I'm going from room to room with the hints in this chapter because that's what you can do when you decide to "go for the green" (as in ecology and saving money) in your house. Mentally or physically, go from room to room and make a list of ways to save our precious natural resources of water and energy.

♦ Save paper and make it easy; write your resource saving list on the inside of a cereal box section and you'll have an instant clipboard to hold while walking around the house.

GENERAL ENERGY-SAVING IDEAS

According to the U.S. Department of Energy, if everyone raised air-conditioning temperatures just six degrees, we'd save the equivalent of 190,000 barrels of oil every day.

If every household in the U.S. lowered its average heating temperatures only six degrees over a 24-hour period, we would save more than 570,000 barrels of oil per day!

If every gas-heated home were properly caulked and weatherstripped, we'd save enough natural gas each year to heat about four million homes.

If everyone scheduled household chores during off-peak hours, the utilities' daily fuel use would be reduced and the nation's energy would be conserved. The reasoning behind this idea is that if everyone did household chores during off-peak times, it would reduce the size of the peak of energy use in the area serviced by a utility company. During peak energy use, utilities may have to meet consumer needs by buying energy from other companies. Also, utility companies have to build plants in sizes to deal with peak use;

in a perfect world where everyone was conserving energy, the power company could build smaller facilities which would then be less costly, not to mention less demanding in fuel use.

Air Conditioning

◆ Change your air conditioner filters often, at least monthly during the cooling season. Don't wait until they are totally clogged. (Neglecting to do this can negate some service warrantees.)

◆ Having the unit professionally cleaned and serviced also increases efficiency. My power company sources say that the maintenance check's cost is easily made up for by savings in energy consumption. It takes a professional to properly oil the condensing unit fan motor, clean the condensing coil fins and condenser fan, inspect the condensing unit for refrigerant leaks, and check the fan control switch. You need to clean the air supply fan motor housing and oil the motor at least once annually.

◆ When walls are cold to the touch, turn off the AC and use fans to move air.

◆ Heavy pollution or plants such as ivy growing on or near the compressor of a central air conditioning unit can cause it to stop up and cool less efficiently. Sometimes units can become so clogged that they burn out the compressor—an expensive repair! Some units can be wrapped with window screen to keep air-borne particles or growing plants from getting into the unit.

◆ Keep your air-conditioning unit cool by shading it with trees, shrubs, or a canopy, and you will get more efficient cooling.

◆ Save energy costs by closing off vents in unused rooms.

♦ It is sometimes more energy-efficient to cool individual rooms with window units than to install several central units to cool different areas of the house. This is especially true for guest rooms that are used only occasionally.

♦ Turn off lights when not in use; they add heat to the room.

♦ Shade windows and glass as much as possible to shut out sun heat.

♦ Don't run attic or window fans when the air-conditioning system is on; you'll be blowing cool air away.

♦ Vent clothes dryer to the outside to avoid adding heat and humidity to the house.

♦ Use ceiling fans to circulate air; it makes you feel cooler. Generally, fans with 36- to 42-inch blades are used in bedrooms and 52-inch fans are used in larger rooms such as living rooms or dens. A ceiling fan uses about the same amount of electricity as a 100-watt light bulb and can allow you to raise the temperature in the house by as much as five degrees while maintaining comfort. For example, if operating a three-ton air-conditioning unit set at 75°F costs you about $550 per cooling season, raising the thermostat to 80°F can drop the operating cost to $399, for a savings of $151 per season.

♦ Cook outdoors or in your microwave.

♦ Dress in light, loose, comfortable clothing, eat light meals, and drink plenty of liquids for personal cooling.

Heating

♦ Check room temperatures with a thermometer; most people are comfortable at 68°F to 70°F.

♦ Open blinds and raise shades to let the warm sunshine in.

◆ Have your furnace cleaned and working parts lubricated before each heating season. Your furnace will last longer and you will have greater heating efficiency.

◆ Gas heaters should be cleaned and adjusted so that the flame is blue.

◆ Close doors and turn off vents to unused rooms that don't need heating.

◆ Electric space heaters are inexpensive ways to heat single rooms.

CAUTION: If you use kerosene or unvented gas space heaters always open a window one inch. Unfortunately, each year we still read about people who suffocate in unventilated rooms heated this way.

◆ If you have wall or window air conditioners that can't be removed for the winter, one way to keep cold drafts from entering the house through the unit is to cover it, inside and out, using a cardboard box that fits over the top, sides, and back part of the unit and a heavy-duty plastic bag that has been fastened on with duct tape.

◆ Insulate electrical wall outlets to eliminate up to 20% of air leakage. You can buy insulating kits for this purpose.

◆ Test your windows for drafts. Light a candle and hold it in front of the window, moving it around the perimeter. If the flame flickers away from the window, you probably need to caulk or weatherstrip them.

CAUTION: Do not put a candle flame too close to flammable curtains or shades.

◆ If your windows allow drafts, you can cut clear heavy plastic (from rolls, drop cloths, clear shower curtains) to measurements slightly larger than the window, then tack the plastic to the wall all around the window. When you want to open the window on a nice day, just remove the tacks from the bottom half, pull the plastic halfway up, and tack it in place. If you put this plastic inside your blinds or window shades it won't be visible from the outside.

Instead of tacking the plastic, in some windows plastic shower curtains or a homemade plastic "curtain" can be installed with permanent or spring curtain rods, then opened and closed as you do curtains.

◆ Place a one-half- or three-quarter-inch foam pad on your mattress in place of the usual mattress pad, and you'll be much warmer on cold winter nights.

◆ An electric blanket allows you to turn down the heat at night and still be cozy.

◆ Insulate your attic to a value of R-19 (often barely enough) to R-30 (the maximum). "R" means resistance to heat flow; the larger the R value, the less heat is lost. If your attic already has four or more inches of insulation, it may be adequate. If you have no insulation, adding six to nine inches of batt or blanket insulation or six to twelve inches of blown-in insulation is recommended.

◆ Wear layers of clothing to trap warm air next to your body, and cover your legs with a lap robe when sitting still.

Heating with Fireplaces and Stoves

The U.S. Department of Energy says that fireplaces are generally inefficient home-heating systems because the open front lets not only combustion gases, but also heat and warm room air be drawn up the chimney and cold air is drawn into the house. Often the damper is left open after the fire dies and then the chimney continues to draw out warm air, resulting in an actual net loss of heat from your home.

Depending upon your fireplace, heating efficiency varies from less than 10% to as high as 70%. If you are buying a new wood-burning stove or building a new home with a fireplace, efficiency should be considered right after safety in your choice.

◆ A heater's efficiency may save fuel. Here is a comparison of the overall energy efficiency of various types of wood-burning appliances from *Buying a Wood-Burning Appliance,* a pamphlet put out by the U.S. Department of Energy's Conservation and Renewable Energy Inquiry and Referral Service. (A heater rated at 10% efficiency requires five cords of wood to produce the same amount of heat as would be produced by one cord burned in a stove of 50% efficiency or by .63 cord in a stove of 80% efficiency.)

1. Traditional open masonry fireplaces—10% to 20%.
2. Masonry plus steel shell circulating fireplaces—10% to 20%.
3. Heat-storing fireplaces and masonry stoves—20% to 60%.
4. Franklin and other open-door stoves (run open)—30% to 45%.
5. Typical circulating stove—40% to 50%.
6. Noncatalytic high-efficiency stoves—60% to 70%.
7. Catalytic stoves—65% to 75%.
8. "Dream stoves" (theoretically possible)—more than 80%.

◆ If you already have a conventional open fireplace, you can significantly improve its heating efficiency and still keep that warm glow you love by installing a fireplace insert to fit. They are usually made of plate steel or cast iron and sheet metal, and can either fit into the fireplace opening or protrude onto the hearth. If they are out on the hearth, they will be more efficient because the top, sides, and bottom will be radiating heat to the room.

CAUTION: Many old fireplace inserts allowed air leakage and creosote buildup in the chimney. The National Fire Protection Association now requires inserts to be installed so that they have a positive connection to the chimney, and that they have a connector between the insert outlet and the first section of the flue liner to send smoke and gases up and out of the chimney. These new regulations increase the cost but make the appliance much safer.

◆ If you are buying a free-standing wood stove, look for clean castings, smooth welds, tight doors, smoothly operating draft controls, and good workmanship. Firebricks or metal plates installed to prevent burnout also increase the "thermal mass" (heat storage potential) of a stove. This means that a 500-pound stove will continue to give off radiant heat for more hours after the fire is out than will a 250-pound stove.

◆ Masonry stoves, such as those popular in Europe, are efficient and safe, but they don't allow for quick temperature control because they are slow to heat and slow to cool. They are also fairly expensive; frequently they are installed when a house is built.

◆ Catalytic combustors for fireplaces and wood stoves are devices that lower smoke emission and increase efficiency. Some stoves and inserts have them built in. They can be installed in existing wood-burning appliances.

◆ Firewood is a renewable source of energy, unlike fossil fuel. Wood varieties that give most heat value per cord (a cord is a pile of wood that's $4 \times 4 \times 8$ feet, or 128 cubic feet) are live oak, shagbark hickory, black locust, dogwood, slash pine, hop hornbean, persimmon, shadbush, apple, white oak, honey locust, black birch, yew, blue beech, red oak, rock elm, sugar maple, American beech, yellow birch, longleaf pine, white ash, Oregon ash, and black walnut.

◆ Here's how to make your fire heat last as long as possible during the night:

    1. Set your furnace thermostat at 55°F to 60°F so that the furnace takes over if your fire goes out.

2. Overheat your room to about 75°F so that if the house cools 15° to 20° by morning, the temperature will still be 60°.

3. Glossy magazine paper has a lot of filler which doesn't burn well and leaves lots of ash. Lay 10 to 15 sheets of magazine paper atop the fire so that it will burn and leave a thick layer of ash to cover the wood. The ash reduces the amount of air that can get to the fuel and slows down the burning rate.

4. Knotty wood pieces that are difficult to chop up make good overnight logs; they will burn more slowly.

5. Close down, but DO NOT shut, dampers to make wood burn longer. The more open the damper, the faster the wood burns.

CAUTION: If you completely shut a damper, gases end up as creosote in the stovepipe or chimney and increase fire risks. Check and clean flues and stovepipes as needed.

6. Add new wood at bedtime and restoke at least once during the night if a stove or fireplace is your major source of heat.

◆ Save ashes for your garden (see "Gardening" section of this book) and to sprinkle on icy sidewalks in the winter.

SAVING WATER, HOT AND COLD

Saving hot water is a double benefit. You save water, and, since heating water accounts for 15% to 25% of the average household energy budget, you also save money on your gas/electric bill. A low or medium setting of 120° or 140°F is usually adequate. The following hints are from various sources, including the Texas Water Board and the U.S. Department of Energy, Conservation and Renewable Energy Inquiry and Referral Service (CAREIRS). You can get the

CAREIRS booklet *Hot Water Energy Conservation and Tips for Energy Savers* by writing the Conservation and Renewable Energy Inquiry and Referral Service (HH), P.O. Box 8900, Silver Spring, MD 20907, or call 1-800-523-2929 from anywhere in the U.S.

Make Plumbing and Hot Water Heater Changes

◆ Repair leaky faucets and toilets promptly. A leaky faucet can waste up to 2,400 gallons of water a year! The next time you have a dripping faucet, put a bucket under it to catch the water and you'll be amazed at how much gets wasted in a day or even an hour.

◆ A leaking toilet can waste as much as 2,700 gallons daily!! Often toilet tank leaks are slow and silent. To check a tank for leaks, flush the toilet; then, after the tank is full, add a few drops of food coloring to it. If water in the bowl gets colored without flushing, you have a leak.

◆ Most toilets use more water to flush than necessary. Save water by placing a sealed brick or an upright open mason jar in the bottom of the tank. Be sure to place it out of the way of any working parts.

◆ Replace standard shower heads with low-flow or flow-restricting ones, which reduce hot water use for bathing by 50%. A shower head with its own on/off valve makes it easy to save water while you're soaping up.

◆ Install aerators in faucets.

◆ If you have a dishwasher that heats water to the necessary 140°F, you may be able to lower the water heater's thermostat setting to 120°F, which is adequate for most families.

◆ If your water heater is warm to the touch, additional insulation, for example from a precut blanket kit for electric water heaters, reduces heat loss.

CAUTION: When installing a blanket kit on a gas water heater, never cover the top or bottom of the heater, and leave a three-inch clearance around the burner and all controls.

◆ Use pipe insulation wrap on accessible hot water pipes to reduce heat loss in transporting the water.

◆ If you are buying a new water heater, look for a tank with at least 1½ inches of insulation and good energy efficiency ratings on the bright yellow EnergyGuide label. Consider the unit's "Energy Factor (EF)," which measures recovery efficiency (how well heat gets to the water), standby losses (how much heat is lost from stored water), and cycling losses. The higher the EF, the more efficient the heater. Electric heaters have an EF between .7 and .95; gas heaters have an EF between .5 and .6, with some as high as .8; oil heaters range from .7 to .85. NOTE: Conventional hot water systems heat water to a specified temperature and reheat it continuously even when water is not being used. Demand water heaters heat water only as hot water is drawn and are rated according to the number of gallons of water per minute that can be raised to a certain temperature. Demand water heaters can't provide large amounts of hot water at the same rate as conventional heaters but can provide enough hot water if used in succession and with water-conserving shower heads or flow restrictors.

◆ Solar hot water systems can provide water temperature of 120° to 170°F, depending on the season and geographical location. The initial costs for solar systems are much higher than for a conventional system; generally they provide about 80% of a family's hot water needs, supplemented by a conventional hot water heater. A U.S. Department of Energy study compared use of solar with use of an electric water heater by a typical family of four and found savings of $5 per month with a solar system, assuming no maintenance cost. Contact you local utility company to relate costs of solar vs. conventional water heating in your area.

General Water-Saving Ideas

In South Texas where I live, drought is a common summer occurrence. We have to conserve water; it's not optional. Many of the water-saving tips in this book come from the Texas Water Development Board.

◆ When you wash your car or boat, consider parking it on the lawn so water runoff gets used by the grass instead of just flowing down the driveway and curb.

◆ When washing a car or boat, attach a spray gun or nozzle to the hose to control water use.

◆ Sweep sidewalks and patios with brooms instead of water from the hose.

◆ Water lawns properly. (See the "Gardening" section of this book.)

Saving Water and Energy in the Kitchen

◆ Put lids on pots to avoid heat waste and help water boil faster—a hint that gives credibility to the old saying "A watched pot never boils!"

◆ Toaster ovens, microwave ovens, and slow cookers use less energy than a range or oven.

◆ When roasting meat, bake potatoes for several meals at the same time. You can reheat stuffed baked potatoes at other meals, saving your time as well as energy.

◆ Today's ovens heat quickly. The old rule of preheating ovens for 10 or 15 minutes wastes energy!

◆ Use small pots on small burners and large pots on large burners for greater efficiency.

◆ Use cool or cold water instead of hot whenever possible.

◆ Keep drinking water in the refrigerator to avoid running the faucet to get cool water each time you're thirsty. It tastes better anyway!

◆ Give each family member a personal jug of water using clean old plastic containers with names or pictures decorating them. Squirt bottles rinsed out with baking soda to remove strange flavors work well and don't spill.

◆ Water plants with water left over from washing vegetables; they also love the vitamins.

◆ Instead of pouring away the remainder of a glass of drinking water, save the water for plants.

    If you keep a plastic container on the counter to collect this water, you'll be surprised at how fast it fills up.

◆ Dishwashers are efficient modern technology helpers. A recent study at Ohio State University showed that on the average, dishwashers use 9.9 gallons per normal load, while hand-washing dishes used from 5.6 gallons to 20 gallons, for an average use of 15.7 gallons. The main cause of wasted water in hand-washing dishes is leaving the water running while you rinse the dishes.

◆ Buy a dishwasher with energy-saving wash cycles, one using less hot water and having a booster to heat available water to higher temperatures. (Air-dry cycles or air-drying dishwasher loads by opening the door also saves electricity.)

◆ Wash full loads in the dishwasher, but don't overload. If you have to hold small amounts of dishes for a few days, you may want to run the rinse cycle or prerinse dishes.

◆ Scrape dishes before loading (I give 'em a wipe with used paper napkins or used paper towels) so you don't have to rinse them; if you must rinse, use cold water. Often, the reason dishes don't get clean in dishwashers unless they are prerinsed is that the water doesn't drain away properly. Having a plumber clear the kitchen drainpipes can make a big difference in dishwasher efficiency—and you'll save water by not prerinsing dishes.

◆ When hand-washing dishes, use a sink stopper or dishpan and run the hot water as little as possible; rinse with cool water. (Add a tablespoon of vinegar to a basin/sink of rinse water to get a clear cool-water rinse.)

◆ Keep freezers full even if you have to fill them with jugs of frozen water (handy to cool food for picnics and for drinking water once thawed). Full freezers recover more quickly after doors are opened and shut.

◆ Clean coils on the back of a refrigerator to improve efficiency by as much as 30%.

◆ Close your refrigerator door on a dollar bill. If you can easily pull a dollar bill past the door seal of the refrigerator door, you need to have the seal replaced to prevent cool air from leaking out.

◆ Keep frequently used items in a handy spot of the refrigerator to save open-door search time.

◆ Side-by-side refrigerator/freezers typically use about 35% more energy than models with freezer on top.

◆ Chest freezers are usually more efficient than upright freezers and are better insulated. If you don't like chest freezers because you hate digging in them, keep certain categories of small food packages (such as vegetable boxes) in supermarket plastic bags. Then, you can move whole units of food instead of lots of small boxes when you are on a search-and-find mission.

◆ Automatic defrost freezers can consume 40% more electricity than those that need manual defrosting.

Saving Water and Energy in the Bathroom

◆ Take a quick shower instead of a tub bath, which uses more water. If you don't believe this, plug the tub for one of your showers to find out how much water you use for an ordinary quick refreshing shower. (Beauty tip: If you plug the tub, you'll be soaking your feet as you shower so that you can give yourself an après-shower pedicure.)

◆ If you have to run water in the shower to get it warm enough to step under, place a bucket in the tub to catch the running water and use it for plants or to flush the commode. (You can do this at the kitchen sink, too.)

◆ When you are adjusting the shower water temperature, turn the hot down instead of the cold up; you won't be wasting excess hot water.

◆ Rinse hands in cold water if they aren't really dirty.

◆ If you are trying to remember to use less hot water (or training a family to do so) invert a margarine tub over the hot water faucet as a reminder. Put a smiley face on it so you don't feel scolded.

◆ When you brush your teeth, turn the water off until it's time to rinse instead of letting water just run down the drain. Some families have a rule that spitting out toothpaste foam must be done into the toilet bowl, which means not having to rinse the sink. Of course, you need not flush a few bubbles of toothpaste foam, which would really waste water!

◆ Hair dryers use less energy when lower temperatures and low air flow settings are used; the bonus is that this is kinder to your hair.

1. Towel-dry hair before using a hand-held or bonnet dryer.
2. If you set your hair in rollers before drying it, wrap small hair sections evenly to allow heat to penetrate more efficiently.
3. If you blow-dry hair, lift and dry small sections at a time and switch to the lower setting when hair is almost dry.
4. For safety's sake, don't leave hand-held dryers on or plugged in when not in use.

◆ Don't use a hair dryer; it's kinder to your hair anyway. I have a friend who has experimented with the air flow in her car and has found that if she opens her driver's side front window and passenger's side rear window by three to four inches and her sunroof, she can get her short, tousled hairstyle from wet to damp driving on the freeway to work. All she has to do is run a pick through it when she arrives. That's natural hair care!

Saving Water and Energy in the Laundry

◆ Wash clothes with warm or cold water when possible.

◆ Pretreat stained areas before loading to avoid rewashing.

◆ Always use cold water to rinse.

◆ Wash full loads whenever possible, but don't overload so that clothing has to be rewashed or have extra rinses.

◆ Always adjust water levels according to load—low, medium, or high. Filling a standard washing machine takes 32 to 59 gallons of water!

◆ Buy a clothes washer with energy-saving features such as moisture sensor control, cool-down cycle, and, if it's a gas dryer, an electric ignition.

♦ Get free distilled water: Strain rainwater through several thicknesses of old, clean panty hose and you can use it in your steam iron or humidifier.

RECYCLING TO DECREASE TRASH OUTPUT

After you make your resource saving list, try to list ways to cut your trash output by one-third or even one-half. See how many would-be discards can be used once or twice more or recycled for another use without a lot of effort.

I learned that I could use a large zippered plastic bag three times without washing it and still have it be sanitary. The first time it held a loaf of bread that had a flimsy wrap; the second time it held a head of lettuce that was partially wrapped in cellophane; the third and last time, it held left-over broiled chicken and was too greasy to save.

Also, if I buy ground gourmet coffee and keep it fresh by placing the paper bags into self-sealing bags for freezer storage, when I finish a bag, I can leave the zipper bag in the freezer (with its scoop) until I buy another; one bag lasts indefinitely.

Get the other side of the cereal box you used for your resource-saving list and use it for your recycling list.

♦ Here's a good tip for grocery shopping: Using cereal-box cardboard for your list lets you prop it conveniently in the shopping cart kiddie seat! Clip "to use" coupons on one corner and used ones on the opposite corner and you'll have no more rummaging through pockets or purse at the checkout.

If you are beginning to see that recycling what might have been trash in your pre-green-awareness life is actually more convenient than it is a chore, you really have the spirit of this book. Read on for more!

DECREASING TRASH OUTPUT IN THE KITCHEN

Food Preparation

♦ Buy mesh reusable coffee filters if they are available for your type of pot so that you don't need paper ones. The health bonus is that unless you use nonbleached paper filters, mesh filters let you avoid chemically treated filters.

♦ You can get one extra use from a coffee filter if you shake the used grounds into a flower bed and then rinse if off and use it instead of your dishcloth to wipe out a grubby ashtray or greasy casserole dish or anything else that's yucky. (By the way, don't substitute paper towels for coffee filters; many of them will break and you'll have a real mess.)

♦ Cool cookies on brown paper grocery bags when you don't have enough racks. They absorb grease, don't need washing, and don't take up permanent cupboard space.

♦ After frying, drain bacon or deep fried foods on brown paper bags with or without newspapers underneath to absorb extra grease.

CAUTION: Drain but don't cook! Some brown paper bags and newspapers are made from recycled paper and can't be used in the microwave for cooking because they may have microscopic bits of metal remaining from the recycling process. Metal can cause the paper to catch fire and possibly ruin your microwave.

♦ If you prefer paper towels for draining bacon, etc., then do it with only one towel, placing newspaper or cardboard from boxes or paper bags under it to absorb extra grease.

♦ If you have drained bacon on paper towels, store the towels in the freezer in a plastic bag or margarine tub. Then use the towels to grease the skins of potatoes before baking.

If you are going to microwave the potatoes, wrap them in the bacon-flavored towels if the towels are microwave safe. Either way it's delicious!

◆ Take a paper plate which has been used as a pot/pan lid in your microwave, fold it in half with the more absorbent underside out, place it as an inverted V in a microwave-safe loaf pan, then drape bacon over it and microwave as usual.

◆ The waxed lining from dry-cereal boxes is heavier than regular waxed paper; use it to line baking pans when you make fruitcakes and quickbreads. Or use it to cover casseroles and other foods in the microwave.

◆ If you wrap potatoes for microwave baking in the lining from cereal boxes, the microwave heat seals the wrap and bakes even very large potatoes faster and with a better texture. You can also microwave corn on the cob wrapped in cereal-box liners. What makes this an even better idea is that the cereal wrap is so sturdy, it won't tear from the steam like regular waxed paper often does. You're less likely to burn yourself and/or mess up the microwave when you pick up the potato or ear of corn!

◆ To grease baking pans and casseroles, you can put a sandwich-size plastic bag into a shortening can and leave it there, ready to insert your hand when you need to grab a blob of shortening for baking.

◆ If you prefer paper towels and salad oil for greasing, the next time you oil a pan, place the oiled towel in a clean margarine tub or zipper-type bag and then into the refrigerator. It will keep for weeks and you won't use a new towel each time.

◆ Keep a nylon net bag made from a clean used panty hose foot filled with flour in your canister so you can flour baking pans or dust a cutting board without making a mess.

◆ Cut or tear newspapers into handy-size sheets, then store them in the kitchen to be convenient when you are peeling or scraping veggies and fruits, chopping nuts, or making other cooking messes that need easy wrap-up and disposal.

◆ Newspapers also line trash bag bottoms so that sharp objects don't poke through causing leaks; they absorb odors in the fridge or freezer (especially when it's being shipped during a move), and make handy wipers-up of kitchen messes.

◆ While it's not recycling, it's good sense to use every smid-geon of catsup, cooking oil, syrup, or salad dressing in the bottle, and you can do this by screwing the caps on securely and storing the containers upside down when they are near empty. You can also drain the remains into the new bottle if you can balance the old on top while it empties itself. And don't forget, you can add a bit of water to rinse out catsup or sauce bottles and then pour the mixture into stews and soups for extra flavor.

◆ Use clean catsup or sauce bottles for homemade salad dressings or for making garlic vinegars and oil. (Put garlic cloves in vinegar or oil and store in fridge for cooking or salads.)

Recycling Miscellaneous Packaging Materials

So many things are overpackaged: a container inside a bag that's inside a box, which may or may not be wrapped with clear plastic. Since starting this book, I have become more aware of waste and when I found a brand of rice that was ridiculously overpackaged at the supermarket, I felt compelled to write to the manufacturer to complain about the waste. Perhaps if more of us refused to buy overpack-aged items, manufacturers would become less wasteful. Aside from waste, overpackaging deludes us into thinking we're getting more for our money just because something comes in a much larger container than needed.

If you've set reduction of your trash output as a goal, you know that just about any washable food container can be reused somehow at least once.

CAUTION: Never reuse containers from household cleaning products, garden chemicals, or any other poisonous substance. When you discard such containers, protect curious children and pets from accidental poisoning. Always seal the lids on tightly and put them into a garbage can with a secure lid. As an extra precaution, you may want to wrap very strong chemical containers in newspaper or plastic bags secured with rubber bands.

◆ Plastic wrap from single cheese slices will separate ground beef patties for freezer storage. They're just the right size.

◆ If you can't get the plastic wrap to stick on a bowl, take one of those rubber bands you've saved from the newspaper or vegetables and slip it over the bowl rim.

◆ The heavy plastic that comes under sliced bacon makes a good minicutting surface and will protect your wood cutting board from odors when you slice onions or garlic. You can also use it to flatten hamburger patties when you are camping.

◆ Save the plates and covers from gourmet frozen dinners, wash well, and then use them to make your own frozen dinners from leftovers or to take dinner to a sick friend.

◆ Some of the plastic plates from TV dinners are even dishwasher safe. Keep them for children's "china," snacks, outdoor eating, or for use as paper-plate holders and plant saucers.

◆ Save the plastic lids from coffee and shortening cans so that you can put a lid from the previous can on the bottom of the new one and keep black marks off your cupboard shelves and dust rings off your counter, if that's where you store them.

• Placing bottles of oils on plastic lids keeps cupboard shelves from getting greasy.

• The plastic lids from two-pound coffee cans are the perfect size for the other half of your breakfast grapefruit. Just place the grapefruit cut side down on the lid, and it'll stay fresh in the refrigerator for the next day.

• If you put mirror film on your windows, you'll have a large piece of plastic that held the film to use as a shelf or drawer liner. If you wish, you can put pretty paper underneath it and the paper will last indefinitely.

• The hard plastic tab that usually holds bread bags or produce bags closed can be a stress saver if you use any sort of self-sticking rolled tape. Just stick the tab under the tape edge after each use and you'll never have to look for the end of the tape again.

• Use a plastic bread-bag tab to save your fingernails when you need to scrape anything, especially pots and pans. It cleans nooks, crannies, and cracks but doesn't scratch non-stick surfaces.

• Plastic tabs can be free guitar picks.

• Large ice-cream and potato chip canisters make good wastebaskets and storage containers, especially when you are moving, because round containers hold plates securely. Sometimes you can get them from ice-cream stores.

• Wash the tiny lidded plastic containers from fast-food catsup, taco, and other sauces, and they'll hold salt for lunches and picnics.

• Clear plastic containers from dates or candied fruits will show off gift goodies you take to neighbors. Just cut out an old Christmas or other occasion greeting card front and paste it over the advertising on the lid.

◆ Any clean plastic container with a tight lid is useful aboard ship for sealing out moisture from tobacco, photos, and watches. Use such containers for mailing goodies to servicemen on sea duty and they'll enjoy the container, too.

Recycling Plastic-Foam Meat and Vegetable Trays

Plastic-foam meat and fresh vegetable or fruit trays can be washed and dried for many practical uses and for craft projects. (See the "Arts and Crafts" section for more ideas.)

◆ Wrap a tray with aluminum foil and place it in the bottom of a silver serving tray to protect it from knife scratches.

◆ Clean plastic-foam trays can be inserted into envelopes to protect photos, computer disks, and other items from being bent in the mail. Make a "box" from two trays placed together bottom side out and secure with a rubber band. They are light and don't add much to the postage cost.

◆ Use the trays for packing material when you mail boxes.

◆ Wrapped with foil or gift paper (recycled gift paper, of course!), they can be used as plates for bake sale goodies or those you give to friends. Some have dividers, which helps you separate candy pieces or different kinds of cookies. Cover with plastic wrap.

◆ Place large foam trays in the bottom of the sink to cushion glasses and china and prevent aluminum and iron cookware from making black marks on the porcelain. Dishes in the water will keep them from floating up.

◆ Cut circles in foam trays or leave them as is if they are the right shape and then place them between china and glass plates, bowls, etc., to prevent chipping and scratching during cupboard storage. Some are flexible enough to let you put cups or smaller items in bowls to save space.

◆ A foam tray under an iron or other skillet will keep black marks off the cupboard shelf.

◆ Cut plastic-foam trays in the shape and size of your feet and use them to cushion and insulate the soles of shoes or nonlined rubber rain boots, especially those children wear.

◆ If the holder for the toilet brush leaks a bit, as some do, put a plastic tray under the brush and also the plumber's helper, if you also store that in the bathroom. You won't have to keep wiping the floor and when it gets messy you can just replace it with another.

◆ Glue a thin circle of sponge or foam dryer/softening sheet on one corner of a large plastic-foam tray to keep the drink container from sweating or slipping and you have a free snack tray children can take outdoors.

◆ Plastic-foam fast-food holders can be used to take individual pieces of pie or dessert to a shut-in or to pack them in a lunch box.

◆ If the plastic-foam holder is deep enough and leak proof, freeze water into large ice cubes for picnics or to float in punch bowls for parties. Float and freeze in ice the last maraschino cherries from the jar or lemon and lime slices to make it pretty and add flavor.

◆ Sturdy foam containers make good drawer dividers to hold hairpins, earrings, and other small items.

Recycling Plastic Bags

◆ If you want to keep a plastic bag liner from slipping inside a garbage can or wastebasket, save the elastic from a rag-bag-candidate pair of men's shorts or panty hose and slip it on as a collar. (You can also use such elastic for tying paper and other bundles!)

♦ Plastic bags are being used in place of paper bags at many grocery stores. Here are some reuses:

1. Hang one on the porch rail, fencepost, or other convenient place to collect ice-cream wrappers, pop cans, and other trash in the yard when children are playing outdoors.

2. When you have several schoolchildren to organize, put each day's clothing in a bag that has the day of the week written on it, then hang all five school-day bags on a hook so each child knows exactly what to wear each day. When children are too big to have foldable clothing, hang accessories and underwear in a bag on the hanger with outer clothing selected for that day and there'll be no morning scrambles.

3. Use them to store newspapers ready for household use, for recycling, or trash collection.

4. Put one over the dustpan when you are sweeping up something gooey or messy. (Sweep with newspaper or second-use paper towels to avoid having a yucky broom in your closet.) You can turn the bag inside out over the mess and discard.

5. And, of course, line small wastebaskets with them so that you can pick up the trash and tie it shut.

♦ Plastic bread bags can be emergency rain boots if you keep a pair in the car. Take off your shoes and put them on instead. You'll protect your good shoes from water damage. Slip plastic bread bags over shoes so that they don't get wet en route, but be careful, don't slip!

♦ Here's a favorite plastic bag tip. If a child who's played in puddles comes in with wet shoes and wants to go back outside, you can slip plastic bread bags or other properly sized bags over dry socks, put the wet shoes back on over the bags, and have a happy child who doesn't have to stay indoors because of wet shoes—and an unstressed parent or sitter, too!

◆ Clear plastic newspaper bags can also be emergency gift wrap for wine or other bottles. Insert the bottle, bottom side down, into several plastic bags, each inside the other. Insert the gift card inside the outermost bag. Pull all the bags up tightly around the bottle neck so that they are smooth and silvery looking, then fasten on top with a bow.

◆ Plastic tube-shaped bags that protect newspapers from rain can be used to store unused rolls of wrapping paper, bows and tags, panty hose and shoes in a suitcase, or to separate different-colored socks and stockings in a drawer and are long enough to keep a stalk of celery or bunches of green onions fresh and crisp in the fridge or a loaf of French bread covered.

◆ Some clothing and household products come in sturdy plastic bags designed to hang up for store display. You can use these to hang and store things in closet, sewing room, or workshop.

Recycling Glass and Plastic Containers

Here's a thought from *Omni* magazine's *Help Wanted: An Activist's Guide to a Better Earth* supplement: We Americans use 2.5 million plastic beverage bottles every hour and we throw away enough glass every two weeks to fill the 1,377-foot-tall twin towers of New York City's World Trade Center!

Glass is one material that can be 100% recycled into new glassware, yet only about 10% is currently being recycled. Also, glass jars are among the most reusable packaging materials we bring into our homes from the supermarket. I always reuse jars to store leftovers, especially because you can see what's in them! They won't get lost.

If you don't keep a special leftovers shelf in your fridge and therefore end up with strange unidentifiable things growing and abandoned in corners, storing leftovers in jars or margarine, cottage cheese, yogurt, or other tubs means you can pitch the whole thing into the trash and not have to deal with something that smells as bad as it looks. The plus is that tossing spoiled foods out in sealed containers keeps them away from curious children or hungry pets and stray animals that may get at your garbage.

When you reuse containers always wash and rinse thoroughly; a vinegar rinse or baking-soda-in-water soak will remove odors left from the previous contents.

◆ Plastic lids from food containers make good outdoor plant coasters. Or put small pots in plastic or other tubs.

◆ Plastic two-liter soda bottles can be adapted for many uses:

1. Cut several in half so that the bottoms will hold celery and carrot sticks upright in the refrigerator.
2. Wash and thoroughly dry one to use as a pouring sugar canister.
3. Cut the bottoms off and use them for snack bowls for children to use while watching TV or playing outdoors or for camping "chinaware" bowls. If they get lost in the sandbox, it's OK!
4. Cut off the tops to use as a funnel. This is especially good if you need a funnel for messy liquids, such as putting oil into your car, or a disposable funnel for pouring paint or household chemicals into a new container when the original is damaged.

CAUTION: It's always better to use original containers, but sometimes bags break or lids get lost. Always label containers with contents if you have to switch from the originals or if you are using them to store homemade cleaning and gardening formulas.

(See the "Gardening" section for more uses for two-liter bottles.)

◆ Plastic pails from ice cream can be reused for many things:

1. Cut a 4-inch-diameter hole in the cover and you have a car trash bucket.
2. With a smaller hole in the lid, it will keep a ball of yarn clean and handy if you knit.
3. Lids alone make good nonreturnable cake plates when you donate to bake sales or potluck dinners or just take goodies to a friend.
4. Buckets can be used as Halloween trick-or-treat collectors, and the bonus is that small children aren't dragging a bag on wet grass and having tragic candy losses when the bottom breaks.
5. Empty laundry detergent into the pail and add a scoop, and you can measure needed amounts without spilling, and take it to the laundromat.
6. Use the pails for kitchen cupboard canisters; they stack nicely and the lids seal contents from insect pests. You can cover them with adhesive-backed paper or leave them as is.

◆ If you're lucky enough to get them, large-mouthed institutional-size plastic mayo or glass pickle jars make terrific cookie jars.

◆ Plastic jugs from bleach, milk, or other products can be cut into scoops with handy gripping handles for dog food, birdseed, potting soil, and other dry materials. Just cut off the bottom. If the plastic is sturdy enough, cut at an angle from the handle to the opposite side of the jug, allowing about an inch of plastic below the handle for support. With less sturdy jugs, just cut off the bottom straight across.

◆ Use the bottom of a gallon jug (with at least one- to two-inch-high sides) for outdoor snacking or plant saucers.

◆ Clean yogurt and dip containers can hold individual portions of gelatin or pudding in the refrigerator, ready for a child's after-school snack or an adult's attack of the munchies. They can also hold canned fruit or other lunch box foods; cookies and chips won't get crushed. If you're a dieter, make individual portions of diet ice cream in cup or half-cup portions as soon as you bring it into the house; then you won't be tempted to overscoop when you have your treat.

◆ Staple several yogurt cups together and you can store paper clips, pins, tacks, and other small items neatly on the desk or in a drawer.

◆ The small, long plastic containers in which tomatoes are sold can be stacked one inside the other for reinforcement and then used inside dresser/kitchen drawers as dividers. They will hold pencils, lipsticks, eye makeup, and in the medicine chest they help organize small bottles and keep them from tipping.

◆ Plastic aspirin bottles can be filled with water, leaving space for expansion, and then kept in the freezer for use as handy small cold compresses for burns and insect bites.

◆ Many medications come in wonderfully useful bottles for holding cologne, hand lotion, liquid soap, or small items for traveling.

CAUTION: Always clean medications out thoroughly before reusing the bottles.

◆ Certain medications that come in bottles with screw lids and sponge applicators can be washed and rinsed well and then used as "lickers" for stamps and Christmas card envelopes.

◆ The plastic containers from wet disposable baby wipes can hold cotton balls, workshop or sewing supplies, or, in a child's room, small soldiers and other toys or crayons and craft supplies. Most of the labels will peel off so you can identify the contents by writing with permanent markers or applying other decorations. Clean thoroughly before use.

◆ After washing, use plastic containers from baby wipes to hold baby's socks and booties on the changing table or in a dresser drawer.

◆ Cardboard powdered infant formula containers are good canisters for dry infant cereal. Keep the scoop that comes with the formula and use it to measure the cereal.

◆ Most scoops from infant formula and other products measure one or two tablespoons; larger detergent measures have cup capacities. If you keep a freebie measuring device in every cupboard canister, you save washing so many measuring spoons and cups when you cook.

◆ One-cup yogurt containers can measure dry ingredients and be reused as what they are—cups. Great for children.

Recycling Glass Jars

◆ Baby-food jars accumulate very quickly and have so many uses; if you have all you can recycle, offer them to a friend who has no babies.

1. Jelly makers love all sizes of baby-food jars: large for fruit preserves; smallest for hot-pepper jellies.
2. Sterilize little jars for freezing snack/lunch box amounts of fruit in the freezer.
3. Everyone's favorite tip is to screw or nail the lids of baby-food jars to the undersides of kitchen cabinets to hold dried spices (either home-dried from the garden or spices that come in fragile plastic

bags), or to the underside of workshop shelves to hold nails, screws, and other small items. They also hold small sewing supplies such as needles and pins. You can use larger jars, too, but baby-food jars are the most popular.

◆ Small spice jars can also be used for home-dried herbs and spices as well as nails, screws, picture hangers, and so forth. Those with shaker tops can be used to hold your homemade mixes of spices or cinnamon sugar for toast, vanilla bean powdered sugar for pastries and other desserts, even vinegar to sprinkle on salads.

◆ Shaker-top jars can hold face powder at home or for travel; attach the powder puff to the jar with a rubber band.

◆ Large glass or plastic jars from mayo or peanut butter are often the perfect size for storing beans, rice, macaroni, cornstarch, chocolate bits, raisins, and powdered or brown sugar to keep them fresh and bug-free. People who do a lot of baking like to keep a vanilla bean in a jar with their powdered sugar so they have flavored "sprinkling sugar." Also, wide-mouth jars stack on each other to save shelf space if you have a pantry.

◆ Pint and quart jars with marked measurements can serve as measuring cups when yours are all in the dishwasher or you are camping. You can measure and mix frothy milk or fruit drinks in them. Two-cup peanut butter jars are especially good for measuring. Mix up homemade salad dressings in marked jars and you don't have to measure oils and vinegar.

◆ Instant-tea jars can be made into kitchen counter sprout growers that are easily irrigated. Punch holes in the lid with a large nail so that you can water your sprouts, replace the lid, and drain the excess. (Use brown bottles for mung bean sprouts because they'll get green if exposed to light.)

To grow sprouts, put about a half-inch of seeds in a large jar, cover with water, and leave overnight. Drain water, irrigate with fresh water, and drain daily for about four days, keeping the jar on its side on the counter, and you'll have plenty of salad sprouts. When the sprouts are ready, irrigate one more time, drain, and put the jar in the fridge to stop growth.

♦ Small jars such as the tiny jam jars from food gift packs and smallest-size baby-food and spice jars can be marked with days of the week and filled with that day's pills to keep track of whether or not you've taken your medication. Line them up in an egg carton or shoe box so they don't get mixed up.

♦ If you take several medications at different times of the day, you can have jars with different-colored lids for the different medication times and just put in the next day's allocation when you take your last pills of the day.

Recycling Aluminum Containers and Foil

Most larger cities have aluminum recycling centers; the amount they pay you for bringing in your aluminum discards depends on conditions in the recycled-aluminum market. Many nonprofit groups use collecting aluminum as a fund-raising device.

About 23 aluminum cans weigh a pound; in some communities, and with some recyclers, that could be about 59 cents that could go to a charity, or into your own pocket, if you prefer. But there are benefits beyond money in recycling aluminum. Some sources say that recycling one aluminum can saves as much energy as it takes to run a TV set for four hours or the energy equivalent of one-half gallon of gasoline.

Garbage magazine (September–October 1989) says that 47% of aluminum packaging and about 15% of steel cans are recycled.

♦ If your city doesn't have an aluminum recycling system as part of regular garbage/trash collection services, you can keep a separate covered plastic trash container in a convenient place, such as outside the kitchen door, in which to collect recyclable aluminum. In some parts of the country, you may need to rinse out cans to discourage unwelcome snackers like roaches or mice from lurking about.

♦ To tell if a can is aluminum, test it with one of your refrigerator magnets. If the magnet sticks to the can, it's not aluminum.

♦ Disposable aluminum pie pans can hold floppy inexpensive paper plates at home, at picnics, or camping.

♦ Use foil pot-pie pans for individual salad bowls or to hold runny foods, cereal, or snacks when eating outdoors.

♦ You'll ALWAYS need to use an oven mitt when you touch them, but in a pinch, aluminum pie pans can substitute for lost pot lids when you are cooking on top of the stove or in a conventional oven.

♦ Bottoms of disposable pie or cake tins can be cut, using an old foil burner bib as a pattern, and used for stove burner guards.

♦ Unperforated aluminum pie pans or grilling trays can be used under house plants. The grilling trays raise small pots out of the drained water, essential for plants such as African violets, which "don't like to get their feet wet."

♦ Aluminum TV dinner dishes or pie tins can be placed under potatoes when you bake them in a conventional oven. The aluminum-reflected heat makes the potatoes bake faster.

The foil covers of frozen dinners are the right size to wrap potatoes for conventional oven baking, for covering some under-the-burner reflector pans on stoves, and for disposable spoon rests at the grill.

◆ Take the leftover too-short-to-cover-anything strip of foil that always seems to get left on the roll and roll it to the thickness of about two pencils, then shape the roll into an "S" and use it to rest chops and other meats on when you grill them. The meat stays out of the drippings. This home-made rack can be washed in the dishwasher and reused, or, if it gets too crusty-burned, you can toss it away.

◆ If you don't feel like making a coil, a loosely crinkled, wadded-up piece of foil (preused or leftover roll piece) can be used to drain bacon and serve as a rack while you keep bacon warm in a conventional oven.

Neat Ideas for Storing Recyclables

◆ Store newspapers and brown paper bags in brown paper grocery sacks. They're the perfect size.

◆ Wrap all plastic wrap from packages around a used paper-towel roll and it will be ready to use in your kitchen.

◆ If you have torn off too much store-bought plastic wrap from the roll or if you have used some that hasn't become messy, stick the wrap on the side of the refrigerator or on the inside of a cupboard door, where it will be handy when you need it. (Some people dunk plastic wrap in the dish water, rinse it, let it dry, and use it again.)

◆ When you store plastic bags, fold or roll them lengthwise from bottom to top so the air is pushed out as you go and then they will be neater.

◆ To avoid having to dig for the right bag, store grocery bags inside a grocery bag, bread bags in a bread bag, newspaper bags inside a newspaper bag, and so forth.

◆ Avoid the aggravation of trying to fit the right lids on bottoms of plastic containers: Before you store them, use permanent markers to mark matching lids and bottoms with stars, smiling faces, or other symbols.

◆ Sometimes, when it's not very messy, aluminum foil can be reused. If you want to do this, place the foil on a level surface and wipe it (gently so it won't tear) with a wet dishcloth or sponge, working from the center out to the edges so it's cleaned and flattened at the same time. Dry it and then reroll on a paper roller or fold to fit your storage space.

◆ Foil for reuse can be stored in the little compartment of some refrigerator-freezer doors, ready for wrapping foods to be frozen.

Brown-Bagging and Lunch-Box Ideas

◆ Any appropriately sized clean plastic tub or glass jar, especially baby-food jars, can hold wet lunch-box treats.

◆ A plastic 35mm film tube can hold sugar, salt, or a lunch-time pill neatly.

◆ Plastic-foam burger holders will keep a salad fresh until noon.

◆ An empty, clean 12-ounce frozen orange juice can will hold soft foods like bananas, cakes, grapes, strawberries, and the like and keep them from being crushed.

◆ Cut a piece from a plastic-foam meat tray and place it in the bottom of a brown paper lunch bag. The bag will stand up. Also, cold foods won't make a "sweat hole" in the bottom.

◆ If you fold up clean wrappers and foil and return them to your brown lunch bag, they'll be handy for tomorrow's lunch if you want to reuse them. But don't save soiled wrappers for washing because keeping them all day at room temperature encourages bacteria growth; you could contaminate food wrapped in them a second time.

◆ The insulated bags some supermarkets use for ice cream make great, free insulated lunch bags.

◆ Have a real lunch bucket. Use a five-pound peanut butter pail after washing it well.

◆ Make a cute lunch bag from outgrown no-cuff pants or jeans that have been worn at the knees. Cut off 12 inches from the bottom of one leg, sew a seam to make a bag on the cut end; the other is already hemmed. Cut off the belt loops and sew them on at the opening so that you can thread a decorative shoelace or heavy yarn through the loops to pull the opening shut. Insert a plastic bag if you need it to be waterproof.

◆ Renew a rusty metal lunch pail by sanding and then spray-painting it. You can add decals to the outside if you wish.

◆ Renew the inside of a metal lunch pail by lining it with adhesive-backed plastic.

◆ When you don't need old lunch pails for lunches anymore you can use them as files for shopping coupons, canceled checks, and recipes; make dividers from cut-up pieces of cardboard from cereal or other food boxes.

These also can be filled with necessities for use as an auto first-aid kit, a toiletries kit for hospital or camping, a doll's suitcase, playthings for a trip to Grandma's or the sitter's, and for storing small children's toys or crayons.

Reuse them as is or spray-paint and decorate them. If converting one to a sewing kit, take a piece of fabric and glue it to the lid after stuffing it with cotton batting, old panty hose, or other material so that you have a pincushion in the lid.

DECREASING TRASH OUTPUT IN THE BATHROOM

◆ If you transfer your shampoo and creme rinse into liquid soap pump dispensers or clean squirt detergent bottles, you won't spill them when groping for them in the shower.

◆ Tie nylon net around used, leftover soap bars to make a diaper pin holder in the nursery. Pins stay sharp, slippery, and safely in place.

◆ Paper cups aren't necessary if each family member has a color-coded or otherwise identified very-own cup. Plastic picnic cups with handles can be hung on a mug rack to keep order.

◆ Burn a match instead of spraying air deoderant, which may contain fluorocarbons, into the air to control odors. (More on odor control in the "Cleanup" section.)

◆ The plastic bags in which some diapers are sold fit some diaper pails perfectly as pail liners.

◆ Take your extra nonmatching washcloths, wet them, and store them in zip-lock bags in the freezer for quick, easily contoured cold compresses ready for your next headache or puffy-eyes discomfort. (Heavy socks or sock tops can be used this way, too, and it's one way to use those nonpaired socks left over when the washer or dryer "eats" their mates or socks with holes in them.) When the "compress" is thawed or warm, return it to the freezer.

◆ Clean all surfaces with baking soda, vinegar, or ammonia (not all three at the same time, though) to avoid using harsh chemical products. (See the "Cleanup and Maintenance Chores" section for more hints.)

◆ Squished toothpaste on the bathroom sink? Take a wet sponge or cloth and use the toothpaste to polish the plumbing or your jewelry.

DECREASING TRASH OUTPUT IN THE LAUNDRY

◆ Remove the round cardboard tube from pants hangers and then bend the ends inward to make a paper-towel holder that will hang anywhere, indoors or out.

♦ If you buy laundry detergent in boxes that aren't large enough for you to dip a scoop into them easily, your detergent will be easier to handle if you transfer it to a clean, dry plastic gallon jug. To pour powder into the jug neatly, use a funnel made from the top section of a clean, dry plastic soda bottle.

♦ If you can, let your washer drain out into your yard; it will water the grass, and the laundry detergent in the water helps to control some lawn pests.

♦ If your washer drains into a utility tub, a stocking fastened over the runoff hose with a sturdy rubber band will keep lint from clogging the drains or septic system.

♦ If your clothes dryer cannot be vented to the outside, use a heavy-duty rubber band, like the kind you find on bunches of broccoli, to hold a panty-hose leg or knee-high lint catcher on the vent pipe at the rear of the dryer.

♦ Don't throw out that fluffy dryer lint! Save it for the spring and put it out in the yard or on a windowsill convenient for nest-building birds.

♦ Used fabric softener sheets have many reuses:

1.   Tuck them in dresser drawers or with linens on shelves to prevent musty odors.
2.   Used foam softener sheets can be used as stuffing for pillows and craft projects such as stuffed animals.
3.   Keep a wad of used sheets handy and use them to clean the screen of the dryer filter; one swipe takes the lint off.

♦ Small paper-towel holders can hold used fabric softener sheets in the laundry room.

♦ Swish a little water around in fabric softener and detergent bottles and you'll be amazed at how much is left in an "empty" container. It's usually enough for a batch of hand laundry, or just pour these smidgeons into the washer.

♦ You may not need to buy a new washer when the tub's porcelain is worn or chipped. Epoxy enamel tub and tile-finish paint can be bought at paint stores and applied according to directions. Think of the hundreds of dollars you save by not buying a new machine, in addition to preserving precious landfill space! (If you think your tub has chips because you're seeing excessive wear on clothing, but can't see the chipped spots, rub an old nylon stocking over all surfaces and it will snag those defects for you.)

DECREASING TRASH OUTPUT ALL AROUND THE HOUSE

Miscellaneous Recycling Hints

♦ Inexpensive plastic-foam ice chests that no longer hold water can be used to store schoolchildren's artworks and papers, sewing supplies, and many other bits and pieces. Felt-tip markers can be used to identify contents. (Don't forget to put names and dates on children's treasures; it's easy to forget whose they are and when they were created.)

♦ Newspapers will absorb water when you have a plumbing flood emergency.

♦ If everyone you know has quit smoking, you can use those ashtrays in many new ways: as spoon rests at the kitchen stove; for plant saucers; catchalls for pins, needles, and jewelry (especially beside your bed so that you don't have to get up when you go to bed wearing earrings or rings you'd rather not sleep in); candle holders (stick candles in bottom-weighted shot glasses and surround the base with non-flammable decorations such as Christmas balls).

◆ Poke pierced earrings into a knit necktie and hang it in the closet or put it in a drawer; you'll always have pairs. You can also use the necktie to hold broaches, pins, and tie tacks.

◆ Don't throw out the telephone book when you move. Take it along for reference when you need to call former associates and businesses.

◆ Cover a phone book (or several phone books together, if yours isn't thick enough) with adhesive-backed plastic or oilcloth or put it into an appropriately sized heavy-duty plastic bag, and then use it for a child's booster chair or step stool. The covered phone book can also be kept under a table or desk as a foot rest for people whose legs don't reach the floor.

Old Panty Hose

Old panty hose have to be the most versatile would-be discards in the house. Keep them in a handy bag made from—what else?—an old panty hose. Some uses are listed here; others are in the "Cleanup," "Gardening," and "Arts and Crafts" sections of this book.

◆ Store panty hose in plastic newspaper tubes and mark the bags according to wearing condition—best, second best, wear with pants 'cause they have a few runs.

◆ Or store panty hose inside old pantyhose. You can color-code your storage so that gray legs hold gray, beige legs hold beige, and so forth.

◆ Cut off the torn leg, then wear two pairs of panties with one good leg on each. It's even warmer that way in winter climates.

◆ Control-top panty hose can be cut at different lengths so that the good parts can be worn. If you cut off from the knee down, the tops can be worn under pants and you can still have bare feet in sandals. Or cut off the feet and keep them in your purse when shopping for shoes during the summer when you're likely to be barefoot.

♦ Elastic waistbands from torn panty hose will hold plastic bags in trash or garbage cans. Just slip them over the lip. Other "rubber bands" can be made from strips cut from control-top panty-hose tops and legs and the elastic bands from the tops of knee-highs.

♦ You can make long strips of strong "nylon twine" if you first cut off the elastic band and then cut through the panty and into one leg and continue cutting in a spiral as you'd peel an apple, all the way to the toe, making a one- or two-inch strip. Then cut strips from the remaining leg. One pair of panty hose will make about 10 yards of one-inch cord for wrapping packages, crocheting into little nylon scrubbers, place mats, or other household items, or for tying up small plants, and many other uses.

♦ Cut about eight inches from the toe and you will have bags in which to tie up and/or hang up all sorts of things. You can hang mothballs in the attic or basement, safely out of children's and pets' reach.

You can boil them to sanitize them, dry them, and then make bags of spices for stew and pickling cucumbers, so that nobody bites a stray peppercorn or bay leaf.

♦ Drop onions or potatoes into panty hose and tie a knot between each one; you can then hang them, clean and dry, for storage. They won't rot as quickly as when they are in a pile or bag, because the nylon lets air circulate.

♦ Braid three strands of three legs each and you have a dog's tug-of-war toy. But, don't let them swallow pieces.

♦ Tie the legs together at the crotch and cut off the remainder of the legs and you have a "hat" to cover your hair when doing messy things like working under a car or in a dusty attic. It keeps long hair out of your eyes and serves as a sweatband. One of these "hats" can also be a nightcap for balding men or a cover for hair rollers.

♦ Tired of combing hair out of your hair brush? Insert the brush into a stocking, press the stocking down with a comb so that the brush base is covered but bristles stick out and then you can quickly clean your hair brush by removing the stocking.

♦ Cut panty hose into small pieces and use them to remove nail polish; they work better than cotton balls or tissue and they are free. (Store in a baby-wipe box, boutique tissue box, or jar.)

♦ Wad up panty hose and stuff them into shoes to keep the toes in shape.

♦ Keep a panty-hose foot in the car and slip it over your "driving shoe" to prevent those nasty black marks and scuffs that get on the back of your accelerator/brake foot.

♦ Old panty hose can be used to tie up stacks of newspapers for recycling.

♦ When you are moving, old panty hose can be used to tie up stacks of books, to tie up flatware without scratching it, to protect and pair skis, and to tie up garden and household cleaning tools and anything else that needs to be tied up or tied down.

♦ Even the packaging from panty hose is useful.

   1. Plastic "eggs" can be made into Easter and Christmas ornaments. (See "Arts and Crafts" section.)
   2. Plastic pouches from some brands are sturdy enough to be mini makeup bags in a small clutch purse. The two-sided tape that keeps the pouch shut can be stuck under a floppy belt end, where it will keep the belt neat all day long.

3. The cardboard sheets some panty hose are wrapped around and the cardboard envelopes some come in make scratch pads, shopping lists, drawing paper, etc. All for free!

Household Paper Uses

Did you know that Americans use about 400 pounds of paper products per capita each year? Compare that to the paper use of the Soviets, who consume about 25 pounds, and the Chinese, who consume about two pounds per capita.

Think about this: A Sunday issue of the *New York Times* uses up the pulp of 75,000 trees, and the average one year's subscription to a daily newspaper uses up the pulp from one acre of forest land. A 35- to 40-foot tree must be cut down to produce only a four-foot stack of newspapers, so if you recycle a four-foot stack of newspapers, you save a tree.

Now, while it's true that trees are considered a renewable resource because new trees can be planted to replace those that are cut down, and the lumber industry and environmentalists are often at odds over how many acres of forest land should be preserved, few people can disagree with the plain common sense of recycling newspapers and other paper; it's wasteful not to recycle it—and there's that landfill space to consider too!

◆ Bits of clean trash paper can be stored in clean paper bags; when the bag is full, squash it and its contents for use as kindling in the fireplace or when camping.

◆ When you buy a large bag of charcoal briquettes, separate them into usable portions for storage in brown paper bags. Fold over the tops to close and then when you are ready to grill, you have a neat bag of briquettes wrapped in its own tinder and you won't have to get your hands dirty. Light the paper with a match and see how quickly you can get started to grill.

✦ Write shopping and other lists, notes, and phone messages on the backs of junk mail paper, cut-up cereal cartons, the 365 small sheets from daily calendar pads, etc.

✦ If you use junk mail envelopes for shopping lists, they can also hold your coupons.

✦ Use the backs of letter-size junk mail for typing drills, children's drawing paper, scratch paper, phone messages, etc.

✦ To avoid confusing recycled scratch paper with letters to be read or kept, staple same-size or cut-to-size pieces together to make scratch pads. One staple in a corner will do. Or draw a line over the printed matter once it's been read.

✦ Use the back of children's drawings and schoolwork as stationery when you write to their grandmas and other doting relatives, so that the treasures are shared.

✦ Use children's extra work papers as stuffing when you mail grandparents' gifts. Of course, never crumple an "A" graded paper! It could escape notice.

✦ Giftwrap that hasn't been crumpled or has been ironed (see "Arts and Crafts" section) can be used to line shelves and dresser drawers. Also, the nonpatterned side can be used for children's drawings.

Cover file folders with leftover wallpaper scraps or adhesive-backed plastic and use them to store household records, newsletters, children's artworks, and so forth.

✦ To make file folders from large cereal boxes, cut off the top and bottom flaps, flatten the box, slit one side; then you can cut off about an inch-width along one long side, leaving about two inches of the length for a tab on which to write the file contents. These homemade file folders hold more papers than store-bought ones.

♦ For magazines, cut off the top flaps and one of the narrow side panels; if you feel ambitious, glue magazine covers on the larger panels to identify the contents.

♦ Cover cardboard boxes for use as file cabinets. Many will hold hanging files and file folders if you don't have bona fide metal file cabinets. And you can write on them to identify the contents!

♦ If you cut the ends of two large disposable diaper boxes and tape them together you can make a file. Cover with adhesive-backed paper or wallpaper scraps to match the room if you wish.

♦ Greeting cards that are so pretty (or so funny) that they must be shared can sometimes be reused. With a card that's folded to four-ply, cut out the inner message page or pages and write on what was the inside of the folded card. With a two-ply card, you can just cut off the message back page and use the opposite side of the picture to write on. Some of these can be postcards, so you can save a few pennies in postage!

♦ Let adding-machine tape continue to roll instead of cutting it off. Reroll it around an empty tape spool, secure with a rubber band, and use the clean side for grocery lists, phone messages, and scratch paper.

♦ Used computer paper is just right to slide under a toddler's bottom when you are changing diapers to keep the changing surface clean. Keep a few sheets in the diaper bag.

♦ Long computer printouts can be donated by businesses to schools (or used at home) for painting, drawing, making long story drawings, and as scratch paper.

DECREASING TRASH OUTPUT IN THE GARAGE

♦ Car antifreeze jugs are made from very sturdy plastic and can be reused for heavy-duty storage of many workshop items after they have been cleaned out.

1. They will hold snow chains neatly in your car trunk if you cut a hand-sized opening in the bottle. (Rub the chain with an oily rag to help prevent rust.)
2. Cut a large flap in one flat surface, line with an old hand towel and fill the jug with car tools, then slip it under one of the car seats.
3. These jugs will hold nails, screws, bolts, and other small but heavy metal objects for garage or work-bench storage.

♦ Fill plastic gallon jugs with sand or cat litter and keep them handy for sprinkling on ice during the winter. Also, many people find it's easier to sprinkle rock salt on icy sidewalks if it's in a plastic jug. And keep a jug of sand or litter in your car for icy emergencies. (A couple of old bath towels or an old blanket can also be used for traction if you are on slippery ice or mud; the bonus is that they are handy if you need to keep your clothing clean while looking under the car in mechanical emergencies.)

♦ Save old tires and lean them against the back wall of the garage to protect the wall and your bumper when you pull into the garage too enthusiastically.

♦ Cut-up pieces of old innertube can be fastened to the supporting pillars in your garage so that car-door paint won't be chipped when the doors are opened.

♦ Hang an old, brightly colored ball, such as a tennis ball, in the center of your garage parking space so you can pull into the exact center. If you hang the ball at the proper distance from the back of the garage to your windshield, you'll know when to stop—the ball will touch your windshield and tell you that you are in the right place.

CLEANUP AND MAINTENANCE CHORES

Mild Cleaning Products

Everyone who reads Heloise knows that vinegar, baking soda, and ammonia are my favorite household helpers. Solutions containing vinegar, baking soda, and ammonia help you avoid complicated chemical cleaners, and vinegar and baking soda are kind to your skin. Vinegar and baking soda are safe for most chores and most people's skins. Ammonia, of course, is stronger and is an irritant; it can burn eyes or skin. Whenever you use ammonia, read the precautions on the label.

CAUTION: Heloise and the Consumer Products Safety Commission emphasize that you should never combine ammonia or ammonia-based cleaners with chlorine bleach when you are making homemade cleaners because the fumes from this chemical combination are dangerous. Always be cautious with any combination of products. Read labels of detergents and cleaners to identify the ingredients; if you are in doubt, call the manufacturer. Most have 800 numbers for consumers to call. You can get the number by dialing information: 1-800-555-1212.

Also, when you use ammonia for any chore, open windows and doors to ventilate the room, and keep children and pets away.

◆ Lightly soiled windows can be washed with several homemade cleaners.

　　1.　Vinegar-based cleaners: Mix one-half cup white vinegar to enough water to make a gallon of cleaner;

or mix one-half cup vinegar, one pint rubbing alcohol, and one teaspoon dishwashing liquid (the liquid used for hand-washing dishes) with enough water to make a gallon of cleaner.

2. Ammonia-based cleaners: Mix one-half cup sudsy ammonia with enough water to make one gallon of cleaner; or mix one-half cup sudsy ammonia, one pint rubbing alcohol, and one teaspoon dishwashing liquid with enough water to make a gallon of cleaner.

CAUTION: Some dishwashing liquids contain ammonia; read the label or call the manufacturer before mixing these with anything. Again, always clearly and boldly label homemade cleaning solutions with the ingredients and keep them out of reach of small children.

These solutions are usually safe on painted surfaces, but it's always best to try a solution on an inconspicuous place first. Mix the solution in a recycled clean gallon jug and then put some of it into an old pump spray container for spritzing convenience.

◆ Many professional window washers say that unless windows are very soiled, they can be cleaned with plain water and a Squeeg-Eze.

◆ If you use full-strength vinegar to clean very dirty windows, you can pour the used vinegar into a tall narrow container, such as a clean dishwashing-liquid bottle, so that the dirt can settle and you can use the clean vinegar again.

◆ You can clean many surfaces with a mixture of vinegar, salt, and water.

◆ To clean fingerprints and built-up dirt from varnished woodwork or paneling, mix one part vinegar to two parts water. Wring out the cleaning rag well and wipe away. After cleaning the wood, polish with a dry cloth to bring out the luster. This solution can also be used on some furniture finishes. Test in an inconspicuous place.

◆ A solution of about half vinegar and half water and an old piece of terry towel will clean finger marks and smears off shiny refrigerators and other appliances.

◆ Pour full-strength vinegar in the track of your sliding glass shower doors, let stand, and then rinse well. Ventilate the room well; full-strength vinegar is not a treat for your nose, even if it does make cleaning easy.

◆ Pour the vinegar water used to clean your coffeepot or teakettle on your rubber drainboard to remove soap scum and lime deposits, or just clean the drainboard with full-strength vinegar.

◆ One-half to one cup of vinegar in rinse water will soften your laundry and cut soap.

◆ If you want to switch from synthetic laundry detergents to soap flakes, which are nontoxic and biodegradable, substitute soap for laundry detergent and add one-third cup of washing soda (sodium carbonate), which helps to remove grease and stains. NOTE: When you first make this switch, detergent residues may react with soap to make your clothes yellow. To avoid this, wash all garments first in pure washing soda to remove the residues.

◆ Make your own spray or more accurately "spritz" starch by mixing two tablespoons of cornstarch in one pint of cold water. Mix and store the solution in a clean spray bottle. Always shake well before using.

◆ Glass and ceramic surfaces can be cleaned with baking soda sprinkled on a sponge, nylon scrubber, or ball-scrubber made from old panty hose.

◆ For a more abrasive cleaner, rub soiled surface with one-half lemon dipped in borax, then rinse.

◆ Kitchen floors and painted surfaces: Soapy film can be removed if you add a splash of white vinegar to rinse water for kitchen floors and painted surfaces.

◆ When you are wiping up dust from plaster or Sheetrock after a remodeling project, add some vinegar to the water and it will speed up the process.

◆ Soapy buildup on chrome bathroom fixtures can be cleaned if you pour a bit of undiluted white vinegar on them and let it remain for about five minutes before you rinse well. For hard-to-remove stains, cover the stain with a tissue and spray with vinegar so that it remains moist for a longer soak, then apply "elbow grease," rinse well, and polish dry.

◆ Lime deposits: Soak shower heads or faucet parts in vinegar overnight to remove hard-water buildup.

Use the same technique to remove rust or corrosion from small objects such as nuts and bolts.

◆ Remove lime deposits from your teakettle by filling the kettle with a mixture of one-half cup each of white vinegar and water; boil gently, rinse well.

◆ Substitute baking soda for scouring powder when you clean (and need to "bleach") kitchen appliances and counters, wooden cutting boards, stainless-steel sinks and chrome plumbing fixtures, refrigerator shelves and drawers, cooked-on grease and oils on cookware and coffeepots, plastic dishes or utensils, and vacuum bottles. The bonus is that baking soda cleans and deodorizes at the same time.

Depending upon how soiled the surface, you can either sprinkle baking soda on a wet sponge or cloth and scrub or make a solution of four tablespoons baking soda per quart of warm water.

◆ Clean shower stalls, tubs, toilets, and tiles with baking soda sprinkled on a damp sponge. Rinse well and buff dry. To clean textured surfaces, apply a baking soda paste, allow to set a few minutes, sponge clean, and wipe dry.

♦ Baking soda paste will clean piano keys—but be careful: Use a small amount and don't let the baking soda fall between the keys.

♦ Easy ways to clean burned pots and pans:

1. As soon as you take the food out, pour water into the pan and return it to the burner to boil for a few minutes or to let it soak using the heat that remains in the burner after you turn it off. For heavier soil, add a small squirt of dishwashing liquid for boiling or soaking.

2. Sprinkle a burned saucepan liberally with baking soda; add enough water to moisten and let stand for several hours, and you can usually lift the burned portion right out.

3. To remove stains from a pan with a nonstick surface, boil a solution of one cup water to two tablespoons baking soda; wipe surface lightly with cooking oil before using it again.

4. To brighten a darkened aluminum pot or pan, boil with cream of tartar in water, or if you have apple peels left over from making a pie or other dish, toss them into the pot with water and let boil.

5. To brighten a blackened or charred stainless-steel pot, try pouring full-strength vinegar in it and then letting it stand for several days; replace vinegar with fresh vinegar and let it stand a few more days. This may be too strong for aluminum or other metals, but it has worked for stainless steel; if a pot is ruined anyway, you don't have much to lose by trying this vinegar soak.

6. If you have no soap pads for scrubbing pots, you can sprinkle some cleanser in the pot and scrub with a loosely crumpled used piece of aluminum foil.

7. Avoid lime buildup in pots used to heat baby bottles or to sterilize home-canned fruits and vegeta-

bles, or in the bottoms of double boilers, by adding one or two tablespoons of vinegar to the water before boiling.

8. Pans won't turn dark when you boil eggs or potatoes if you put a small amount of vinegar in the water. A small amount doesn't affect the taste but does brighten the pan.

♦ If you hand-wash dishes, adding about a half cup of vinegar to the dish water will keep grease from clinging to dishes, pots, pans, and the sink.

♦ Apply a baking soda paste to grease stains on wallpaper (IF IT IS WASHABLE) and allow to dry. Brush off with a soft clean cloth or brush.

♦ Baking soda on a wet sponge will remove crayon stains on washable painted walls. Apply and scrub gently.

♦ To clean and deodorize a toilet: Pour in undiluted white vinegar, leave it for about five minutes, then flush. Stubborn hard-water stains can be scrubbed with undiluted vinegar.

If you have lime deposits on the toilet bowl above the water line, line the bowl with three or four thicknesses of paper towels (used previously for hand drying) and pour vinegar over the towels to saturate them. You may have to add vinegar to keep the paper moist until the deposits dissolve and you can brush the toilet clean again. (The same technique also works for sink fixtures that have lime deposits; just wrap them with paper towels and proceed as you did with the toilet bowl.)

CAUTION: Don't flush paper towels down the toilet. They can clog the drain.

Another way to clean the toilet bowl is to scrub it with baking soda and a toilet brush.

♦ You can deodorize and disinfect bathroom surfaces by wiping them with a solution of one-half cup borax to one gallon of water.

◆ Baking soda deodorizes diaper pails and musty places. To deodorize shoes, sprinkle baking soda in them and shake out the powder before wearing.

◆ Plastic shower curtains can be renewed if you wash them in the machine with a towel; add one cup of white vinegar to the rinse cycle and tumble-dry briefly.

For quick removal of soap film and mildew, pour full-strength vinegar on the shower curtain and then rinse.

◆ Clothing stains: Remove deodorant and antiperspirant stains from some clothing by rubbing the stain with white vinegar before laundering.

◆ You can remove most cola, wine, and ketchup stains from 100% cotton, permanent press, and cotton blends if you sponge with undiluted white vinegar within 24 hours. Then launder or dry-clean according to manufacturer's instructions.

◆ If you keep vinegar handy in a clean squirt bottle, it's easy to saturate stains or use it for cleaning.

◆ Carpet stains: White vinegar mixed with one teaspoon of mild liquid detergent and one pint of lukewarm water will remove many oily stains from carpeting. Apply mixture to stained area and rub with soft brush. Rinse with towel dampened with clean water; blot well to dry.

◆ Upholstery and rug surfaces can sometimes be freshened and minor soil removed if you sprinkle on dry cornstarch and then vacuum it up. Add a touch of cinnamon.

◆ To freshen carpets, sprinkle dry baking soda onto the carpet with a flour sifter, let it remain on the carpet for about 15 to 20 minutes, and then vacuum.

◆ Baking soda can absorb odors and help remove stains from mattresses that have been wet. Remove bedding from the wet bed, sprinkle mattress liberally with baking soda, let set 12 to 24 hours, and remove baking soda with a vacuum or whisk broom.

◆ To remove odors from your hands, rub with lemon juice and wash as usual, or rinse them with vinegar.

◆ Vinegar will get rid of that slick feeling you have on your hands after using household bleach products or giving yourself a home permanent. Wash your hands with soap and water, rinse, then apply vinegar.

◆ Adding one-half cup of white vinegar to the rinse water when you wash clothes will remove soap traces and make dark clothing look bright and all clothing smell fresh.

By the way, cider vinegar applied full strength to a clean scalp when you wash your hair imparts a sheen and in some cases controls dandruff.

CAUTION: Take care not to get the vinegar in your eyes, and if you have sensitive skin, consult a dermatologist before using this tip.

◆ To make a whole room smell better, put some vinegar, a few cloves, and a little cinnamon in small glass jars, put the jars in the microwave for a minute or so and then place them where needed. This seems to absorb odors rather than just covering them up like a commercial room deodorant spray—and it doesn't put fluorocarbons into the air, as do some sprays.

◆ To remove solidified egg yolk from a plate or gooey cheese left from a dish like lasagna, sprinkle the stuff with salt before washing and it will come off easily.

◆ To clean brass: Dissolve one teaspoon of salt in one cup of white vinegar and add enough flour to make a paste. Apply this mixture to the brass and let stand for about 10 minutes. Rinse the object well with warm water and polish dry.

◆ To quick-clean copper or brass: Saturate a sponge or cloth with vinegar or lemon juice, sprinkle salt on the sponge, and then lightly rub, rinse, and dry. Or dip a used half of lemon in salt and scrub away.

This won't take burned stuff off copper-bottomed pans, but it will shine the copper.

◆ Here are two ways to clean silver—but CAUTION: Home-style methods can leave a dull white luster and remove the dark accents (patina) in design crevices. They may also soften the cement of hollow-handled flatware. Use only for badly tarnished pieces that are not of very high value.

1. Place aluminum foil in the bottom of a cooking pot. (Aluminum pots may get darkened if used for this process.) Add enough water to cover the silver pieces. For each quart of water, add one teaspoon of salt and one teaspoon of baking soda. Bring solution to boil. Add silver. Boil one to two minutes. Remove silver, rinse, and buff dry with a soft cloth.
2. A quicker way to do this is to put a piece of aluminum foil at the bottom of the kitchen sink, fill the sink with very hot tap water, and then do the rest of the procedure described above.

◆ Keep drains clear with this method instead of using harsh caustics:

Each week, pour one cup of baking soda into the drain, followed by one cup of vinegar. As the soda and vinegar foam, flush the drain with very hot water. This is designed to keep kitchen or bathroom drains clear.

If you have a plugged drain that can't be opened with a plumber's helper, call the plumber. Caustic chemicals won't unclog a badly stopped-up drain, and if sewage mixed with caustic chemicals backs up into your sink or tub, the surface glaze can be damaged. Then it will stain very easily and seldom look clean unless bleached frequently.

◆ Keep a bottle (a clean old squirt bottle is helpful) of plain white vinegar in your car and some paper towels or rags so that you can clean grease off of your windshield.

◆ Sliced white bread is a handy cleaner—and it's nice to know that it's good for something.

1. You can clean some types of wallpaper by rubbing the dirty area with a wad of plain white bread.
2. Here's how to restore a sheen to old books: After placing the book on a flat surface, lay a piece of fresh white bread on top of it and then roll the bread over the entire surface of the book with the flat of your hand. It may take two or three slices per side of the book, depending upon how dirty it is. Don't forget to rub the back strip with the bread. While this doesn't restore color or remove bad mildew stains, it does restore a sheen to old books, which of course can't be cleaned with any type of liquid.

Cleaning Equipment

◆ We used to recommend newspaper for washing windows, but the type of paper and inks used today are not exactly the same as they used to be when we began this column. Not all newsprint is absorbent enough and some of the inks smudge on the window casings. You'll have to test your local paper to find out whether it can be used for cleaning.

◆ Bring back the rag bag instead of using paper towels for everything. To store rags, put an old T-shirt on a sturdy hanger, knot the bottom shut so that you can toss socks, underwear, panty hose, and other rags into the neck opening, then hang in a convenient place.

◆ Fill a clean, dry squirt bottle with baking soda so that you can squirt the baking soda on smelly wet rags such as dishcloths and washcloths. They will smell fresh and clean.

◆ Hang a small hand towel or large washcloth on a cup hook next to your paper-towel roll so that you won't use a disposable towel all of the time. Sometimes the label is a hanging loop. The rule in my house is that clean hands get wiped on cloth towels; paper towels are used only for messy, icky things.

◆ If you want to stop using paper towels completely, save the last roller and use it to hold a small terry towel. Also, you can make a tube by folding one end of a terry towel over the other and sewing it, or make a tube from two small hand towels, then insert the paper roller and replace the roller in the holder.

◆ Don't rip off the paper towel each time you dry wet but clean hands; let it hang so it can dry for reuse.

◆ Paper towels from drying clean hands or wiping glasses, mirrors, and other non-icky things can be reused for really dirty jobs. Tuck them in with your cleaning tools and supplies or have a basket on the kitchen counter or windowsill to keep them handy.

◆ You don't always need a whole paper towel, especially if you buy towels that are about one-third longer than normal (but still have the same total length on the roll!). Rip the end section in strips to the perforations, then hold on to the whole roll while you rip off just a strip for small wipe-ups.

Or when you start a new roll, cut the roll in half with a sharp knife before you unwrap it without cutting through the paper roller. Then you have two small rolls side by side that are good for little cleanups and make your roll last twice as long.

You can cut through the paper roller and have two small rolls and still hang them if you buy an inexpensive bathroom tissue holder—the kind that have a lightweight metal frame and a wooden roller—and mount it in your kitchen.

◆ Hang a clothespin bag on a kitchen cupboard knob to hold reusable paper towels and small wiping rags.

◆ If you use crumpled paper towels and napkins to wipe dishes before putting them into the dishwasher, you won't waste water prerinsing them.

◆ Cardboard rolls from paper towels or toilet tissue can protect your fingers from knife blades stored in a drawer; flatten them and insert the knife. You can staple the ends and sides to get a better fit.

◆ If your kitchen drawer organizer keeps sliding back and forth, a cardboard roll cut to fit the empty space will brace it in position.

◆ Roll ribbons, scarfs, veils on cardboard rolls to keep them stored without wrinkles.

◆ Old panty hose—whole ones or parts of them—made into balls shine chrome bathroom and kitchen fixtures, scrub sinks, tubs, and woodwork, and are perfect for washing the car: You can scrape off dirt blobs without damaging the paint.

◆ Fit a pair of panty hose over a broom to dust walls, ceilings, and baseboards.

◆ Can't find a rubber glove to pick up something messy? Poke your hand into a heavy-duty plastic bag and grab.

Home Maintenance Chores

◆ Use water-base instead of oil-base paints; they release fewer toxic fumes. Always keep windows open when you paint.

◆ When you are selecting a paint color, buy a small can and try painting a large piece of cardboard carton with it, so that you can get a better idea of the color's aesthetic impact. This is an especially useful hint if you are matching paint to wallpaper, for a little chip just doesn't tell you much.

♦ When you are painting the wooden strips around window-panes, cut newspapers into long, one-inch strips; dip each strip in water; gently pull strips between your thumb and forefinger to remove some of the water and then press the strips onto the windowpanes close to the woodwork. Do only two panes at a time. As soon as you've painted a section, remove the paper. You won't have any sticky masking tape residue to get off the windows with this method.

♦ Drape newspaper over the top of a door to keep splatters of paint off it. Also, if you are working on a ladder on one side of the door, write a message on the draped newspaper telling someone on the other side of the door to be cautious about opening it. You could prevent a ladder-fall accident.

♦ If you are painting on a ladder and can't send playing children and pets to another planet until you are finished, avoid messy paint spills with this system: Fasten an inverted plastic lid of a coffee or shortening can to the bucket shelf of your ladder with carpet tacks. Then pour paint into a smaller clean can, filling it with as much as you dare. Set the can into the inverted lid and you can even move the ladder without spilling paint.

♦ Instead of spray-painting wire fencing or metal lawn furniture, which pollutes the air and wastes paint at the same time, wear a rubber glove and use a sponge dipped in paint for no-mess easy application.

♦ Strain paint through old panty hose stretched over a rounded wire coat hanger.

♦ When you are storing paint, it will keep a long time if you pour it into a gallon-size milk jug. The advantage is that when you need to touch up a mark on the wall, all you need to do is shake the jug well and pour some out into a margarine tub or on a sponge; you don't have a mess. Mark the jug clearly with contents and the paint's color code, just in case you need more.

◆ Place a piece of newspaper over a paint can before you put the lid on, then hammer the lid in place. It seals the can and prevents paint from splashing on you.

◆ To clean brushes after painting, pour paint thinner into a baby-wipe container; the paintbrush will hang from the slot in the lid and the bristles won't get bent as it soaks. You can also use the time-honored way of cutting a slot in the plastic lid of a coffee can to hold the brush as it soaks in the can.

◆ Wipe paint rollers on old newspapers before cleaning; it's easier when there's not too much excess.

◆ To keep the garage floor from getting painted when you are spray-painting a craft project, place the object in a large cardboard box. It will contain much of the mist. Use this tip when painting on driveways, patios, and grass.

◆ Use solid wood when doing home construction. Formaldehyde emissions from plywood and particleboard are indoor air polluters.

◆ Instead of using sprays, lubricate hinges, doorknobs, locks, and latches with castor or mineral oil. (Salad oil tends to get rancid, so don't use it for this purpose or to reoil wooden chopping blocks or salad bowls.)

◆ Use rechargeable batteries instead of disposable ones. Batteries corroding in landfills contaminate our underground water supplies with cadmium, mercury, and lead. Take used disposable batteries to a household hazardous waste collection day, if your community holds them.

◆ Barbecuing pollutes the air, no matter what you do, but you will be doing your best to control pollution if you light the coals with kindling instead of lighter fluids and avoid using self-lighting coals.

Household Pests

◆ Lizards are considered good luck in some parts of the world, and with good cause: They eat insects. If one gets trapped in your house, you can get it back outdoors where it belongs without hurting it. Throw a large piece of nylon net over the lizard; it will get stuck in the net and then you can scoop up net and lizard and shake it outdoors.

◆ Ants love to munch on any food left out, especially those containing sugar. To avoid being hospitable to ants:

1. Don't leave food out overnight, and keep all work surfaces clean.
2. Keep food in your refrigerator or freezer, or in sealed containers.
3. Wash kitchen floors frequently so that spills don't attract food-seeking insects.
4. Take trash out each night or at least keep it near the door so that insects don't do a whole house tour to get at the trash.
5. Keep the perimeter of your house free of dense plants, woodchips, and other things that encourage breeding of ants and other pests.
6. Plant mint around your house perimeter. Ants don't like it.

◆ When your pet has fleas, your house has even more fleas, since only about 20% of the fleas are actually on the animal. The rest are in carpets, upholstery, and corners, merrily breeding more generations to vex you and your pet. Also, fleas can jump 12 inches or more in one leap, but then you probably noticed that if you have pets. Here are a few non-chemical flea remedies:

1. Keep fleas off you by bathing in soaps that contain certain green dyes that repel fleas. At least one hand lotion also contains the flea-repelling dyes.

2. Toss a couple of mothballs into the vacuum cleaner bag before cleaning and the fleas will die when sucked into the bag.
3. Make a flea trap by placing a light-colored shallow pan of soapy water on the floor next to a 25-watt lamp with the bulb about one or two feet above the water. Leave the lamp on overnight with no other lights on in the room. Fleas are attracted to light, will jump toward the heat, and fall into the pan and meet their demise by soapsuds.
4. Wrap sticky tape, sticky side out, around your hand and dab up the fleas you can see.
5. Some people swear that cedar shavings in pet pillows repel fleas.
6. Dust powders made from eucalyptus, sage, tobacco, wormwood, sassafras, bay leaf, or vetiver on your pet.
7. Mix essential oils such as citronella, cedarwood, eucalyptus, pennyroyal, orange, sassafras, lavender, geranium, clove, rue, or mint with water and use for dips and shampoos on your dog. For shampoo, mix one-half teaspoon essential-oil repellent, one teaspoon shampoo, and one cup water.
8. Adding a bit of brewer's yeast or onion or garlic salt (not all at the same time) to pets' food has been reported to make some animals unappealing to fleas, but there is no scientific evidence to prove this.

CAUTION: Garlic can give pets diarrhea and bad breath, and too much of it has been known to cause blood disease.

♦ Moths lay their eggs on woolen and silk fabrics and furs so that the larvae will have food when the eggs hatch. Prevent moth damage by dry cleaning or washing garments before they are stored. Cedarwood repels moths. Dried lavender flowers are an old-fashioned moth repellent and they leave a scent much more pleasant than mothballs.

◆ Roaches are most adaptable. It has been estimated that more than 10,000 cockroaches can live and reproduce beneath your refrigerator during a 12-month period, even if the rest of the house is immaculate! Yuck!!

1. Keep roach hiding places clean: sinks, old product boxes, closet water heaters; the insides of all appliances and radios, wall clocks, TV's, and stereos; cupboards and drawers; cracks in plaster and at baseboards. Seal the space around waterpipes under your sink with duct tape to keep roaches out.
2. Roaches love the glue in cartons, brown paper bags, and even your wallpaper. Serve them as little as possible by storing cartons and bags in the garage or carport.
3. If you don't want to use commercial insecticides, try Heloise's Famous Roach Recipe, which has been used successfully by hundreds of thousands of Heloise readers. For over 30 years.

CAUTION: Boric acid can be poisonous to small children and pets. Keep out of reach.

Heloise's Famous Roach Recipe

¼ cup shortening or bacon drippings
⅛ cup sugar
8 oz. powdered boric acid
½ cup flour
½ small onion, chopped (optional)
Enough water to form a soft dough

Mix the shortening and sugar together until they form a creamy mixture. Mix together the boric acid, flour, and onion, then add to the shortening-and-sugar mixture. Blend well, then add water to form a soft dough. Shape the mixture into small balls, or just drop blobs into open plastic sandwich bags to keep it moist longer. Make sure you label the bags clearly so that everyone in the house knows it's a roach lunch and put in out-of-the-way places. When the dough gets hard, replace it.

Dry Powder Mixture

Mix equal parts of boric acid and one of the following:

Flour
Cornmeal
Sugar

Use for dusting infested areas. Cockroaches walk through it and then ingest it when they groom their legs and feelers.

Boric acid can be obtained at drugstores, pharmacies, or grocery stores. For larger quantities, buy it from wholesale chemicals distributors.

♦ Silverfish and firebrats like materials that are high in protein, sugar, or starch, such as cereals, flour, paper with glue on it, or starch in clothing and rayon fabrics. Here is a home bait recipe:

Silverfish Bait

1³/₄ cups oatmeal ground to flour in a blender
¹/₂ teaspoon granulated sugar
¹/₄ teaspoon salt
¹/₄ teaspoon barium carbonate or sodium fluoride (from pharmacies or chemicals supply houses)

Mix thoroughly and put about one teaspoonful each in several shallow boxes near insect hiding places. Cover each box with a crumpled piece of paper. Results will take two to three weeks.

A variation of this recipe: Mix one cup of flour with five teaspoons of sodium fluoride and apply like the bait above.

◆ If you don't want to make your own roach killer, use insecticide-containing roach traps instead of sprays, which may contain neurotoxins such as chlorpyrifos.

◆ Weevils can be so tiny that you can hardly see them. Prevention is the best solution to weevils in your cupboards.

1. Check foods before putting them away to make sure you aren't inviting weevils to your cupboards.
2. Store products in glass jars or tightly sealed plastic bags to prevent contamination.
3. When you bring grain products home from the market, first place them in your freezer for four days or in the oven set at 150° to 160°F for 30 minutes to eliminate weevils and weevil eggs that could be in them.
4. Buy only enough staples to last a few weeks. Weevils are more likely to invade long-stored products.
5. Some readers claim that sprinkling black pepper or putting bay leaves or unwrapped sticks of spearmint gum on pantry shelves deters these pests.

◆ Spiders feed on all types of insects and so are helpful, but we still don't like them indoors. The webs are a nuisance indoors and can be brushed or vacuumed away.

◆ Mosquitoes lay their eggs in or near water because their eggs need moisture to hatch. Clean out birdbaths and fountains regularly and don't leave containers around that will hold rainwater and thus provide places for mosquitoes to lay their eggs.

◆ Houseflies and other flying insects can spread diseases. Their larvae, called maggots, live in garbage, sewage, soil, water, living or dead plants, and food left out.

1. Keep screen doors closed to keep flying pests out of the house.
2. Keep all food covered or tightly sealed.

3. Wrap food you throw away so that trash cans aren't an insect buffet.
4. Keep a squirt bottle filled with water and a bit of mild dishwashing detergent near the kitchen window so that you can squirt flies or gnats—you'll kill them and wash windows at the same time!
5. Hair spray will stop a flying insect in flight.
6. Since flies tend to mate in the center of the room, hang flypaper there instead of at the corners. It won't be attractive, but it will be more effective.
7. Make home-style flypaper with honey applied to yellow paper. Hang the paper from the ceiling. The color will attract the flies and the honey will hold them.

◆ Indoor plants with bugs can be helped if you mix a few drops of dishwashing liquid and warm water, put the mixture in a spray bottle, and spray leaves weekly. Don't use this on flowers.

If you dip a cotton-tipped swab in alcohol and dab plant areas affected by mealy bugs, it should get rid of them. Do have a light touch and be careful with tender young leaves because alcohol can burn them.

◆ Get rid of ants with boric acid; prevent them from returning by planting mint or onions, which are insect-repelling herbs, around the house.

Section 2
Outside the House

GARDENING

Organic gardeners used to be considered almost members of a cult. But now that we know how chemical fertilizers and pesticides affect the environment we humans and our wildlife live in, "organic" has become one of the key words of the green movement.

We are aware of the effects of overfertilizing and pesticides on our water supplies, the food chain of wildlife, and wildlife itself. People fear that soil erosion will bring back the dust bowls and economic destruction of times past. Planting more trees and regulation of forest use and of burning fossil fuels has become important because we fear the much publicized "greenhouse effect" and climate changes resulting from it. Concern about "clean food" without pesticide residues has made gardeners out of people to whom a spade was something found in a deck of cards, not in their garage with the rest of their gardening tools.

Here are some tips for gardening, from various sources, that use home remedies and recycled household material.

Lawns

Not only does your lawn cool the air by releasing moisture and reflecting 40% to 50% of the sun's rays, 5,000 square feet of healthy lawn also produces daily, through photosynthesis, enough oxygen for a family of four. You can have a healthy lawn without excessive use of chemicals. Here are the 9 steps to a healthy lawn published in an article by Peter H. Johnson of Rodale's *Organic Gardening* magazine.

1. In the spring, use a bamboo or spring-steel leaf rake (not a heavy metal rake such as is used to prepare a garden seedbed) to remove leaves, trash, old grass, and other litter. Some of this material can be put into a compost pile and used for mulch after it has decomposed.

2. If you see insect, weed, or disease problems after cleaning up your lawn, you may be able to solve them without chemicals. For example, some areas of your lawn may have patches of mold under dead leaves and clipping, or moss, which means poor drainage and fertility. Both of these problems can

be solved by allowing more sun to shine on the affected areas. Lawn diseases such as dollar spot, snow mold, or brown patch can be discouraged by setting your mower about one and a half to two inches higher, so that new growth can occur, and by aerating the areas with vigorous raking.

3. Get a soil test from a local garden center or your county's Cooperative Extension agent. It will be listed under the county name. There may also be a U.S. Department of Agriculture Soil Conservation office in your area. Look in the phone book under "United States Government." A soil test will tell you if you need to change your fertilizing and watering habits.

4. Aerating the soil has been shown to reduce thatch density and help the soil hold and release plant nutrients. You can rent an aeration machine from a garden center.

5. Feed your lawn with the same organic fertilizers you feed the rest of your garden. Cottonseed meal, castor bean pomace, blood meal, composted cow manure, and compost are good nitrogen sources. The best times to fertilize a lawn are spring and fall.

6. Mow properly according to the type of grass you have. Also, it's better to mow lightly and frequently than heavily and infrequently, because there's less stress on the grass. Most experts agree that you shouldn't cut off more than one-third at a mowing. Set the mower blades higher and mow less often in the summer. Letting grass grow up allows roots to grow down and tolerate dry spells better. Mow one-half to one inch higher in shady areas so that there is more leaf surface for photosynthesis in the low light.

7. Water enough to give the subsoil a good supply, which means watering until you hear a slurpy

sound when you walk on the lawn. Inadequate daily watering just wets the ground surface and causes shallow root growth. Night watering won't cause diseases if you water heavily only once weekly. Keeping the grass wet encourages diseases.

8. After you've corrected the cause of a bare spot, reseed it by placing a bushel of topsoil on your driveway and mixing in five pounds of organic fertilizer and one pound of grass seed. Mix thoroughly and toss handfuls of the mixture onto the bare patch, then rake lightly and cover with straw or moist burlap. Keep the reseeded area damp for three weeks to allow sprouting.

9. Weeds seldom grow in healthy lawns because grass crowds them out. If you have weed patches, dig them up with as much of their roots as you can and then reseed as described above. Crabgrass or quack grass won't tolerate shade, so you can get rid of such patches by covering them with a tarp or black plastic sheeting for two weeks. Although your lawn may look bleached and discolored, it will recover—but the crabgrass will have died.

The Public Citizen Congress Watch (PCCW) is a nonprofit organization that has prepared material about lawn-care pesticides and offers a two-part report entitled *Keep off the Grass.* One part is "State Regulations Covering the Lawn Care Industry" ($8) and the other is "A Survey of Health Effects of the Most Commonly Used Lawn Care Pesticides" ($5). Obtain this information by contacting PCCW at 215 Pennsylvania Ave., SE, Washington, DC 20003; phone: 202-546-4996.

PCCW says that if you decide to have your lawn treated by a commercial lawn-care firm, you should ask about the chemicals to be used. Of the 30 different pesticides commonly used on lawns, at least 10 are known or suspected carcinogens (cancer-causing agents). The suspected or known carcinogens used on lawns include the following (brand name is given in parentheses):

Insecticides: Acephate (Orthene), Baygon (Propoxur), Carbaryl (Sevin)

Fungicides: Benomyl, Chlorothalinol (Daconil)

Herbicides: 2,4-D; Glyphosate (Round-Up), MCPP (Mecoprop), Pronamide, Oxadiazon (Ronstar).

There is a class of pesticides called organophosphates, which can have other, more immediate, health effects, including such symptoms as headaches, dizziness, weakness, muscle twitching, nausea, diarrhea, and sweating. More severe poisoning can lead to tremors, convulsions, respiratory arrest, and even death. The organophosphate pesticides used on lawns, all of which are insecticides, include Acephate, Chlorpyrifos (Dursban), Diazinon, Malathion, Isofenphos (Oftanol), Isazophos (Triumph).

Some safe commercially available organic fertilizers for your lawn and garden include Fertrell, Erth-Rite, and Ringer's Lawn Restore. Compost, which you can produce by allowing various organic materials to decompose (leaves, grass clippings, woodchips, and kitchen scraps such as peels, coffee grounds, egg shells, etc.), is an effective lawn fertilizer. Your Cooperative Extension agent can help you answer composting questions appropriately for your area. (Also see the information on composting in this section.)

Starting a Healthy-Planet Garden from Scratch

Here are some tips from the EPA on starting a garden:

1. If it is a new plot of land, find out how the land was used previously so that you'll know if chemicals have been applied or if runoff from a neighbor's pesticide use will put residues on your produce.

2. If the garden plot is already established, residues from previously applied pesticides can remain in the soil for many years; you may want to speed up the process of removing them by planting an interim nonfood crop such as annual rye grass, clover, or alfalfa. The roots of these crops will take up some of the pesticide residues. Discard these crops without working them into the soil and continue to alternate food crops with cover crops in the off-season to continue this pesticide-removal process.

3. When nothing is growing in the plot, on sunny days turn over the soil as often as every two or three days for a week or two to allow the sunlight to break down some of the pesticide residue.

4. Build and feed the soil with compost and manure so that healthy crops will grow in it.

5. When you plan your garden, select hardy, disease-resistant varieties of fruits and vegetables so that your pest control will be minimal.

6. Alternate rows of different kinds of plants to prevent pest problems from developing.

7. Rotate crops yearly to keep plants from being damaged by pests that live from season to season.

8. Mulch the garden with leaves, hay, grass clippings, or shredded or chipped bark. Mulch retains moisture and keeps weed growth down.

9. Learn how to manage pest outbreaks without chemicals.

Home-Style Remedies for Your Yard

Here are some home remedies for better gardening that don't include harsh commercial chemicals:

◆ If you pour full-strength vinegar or salt on unwanted grass growing between sidewalk cracks, it will die off.

◆ Clean and shine the leaves of large houseplants by wiping them gently with a soft cloth (old T-shirt or other cotton knit scraps work well) that has been dipped in a solution of one-fourth to one-half cup of white vinegar per gallon of cool water.

◆ "Skunked" in the garden? Don't bury your clothes. Soak them for several hours in a solution of one-half cup baking soda or vinegar and one gallon of water, then wash.

◆ If you get sticky sap on your hands and clothing after pruning certain trees, rub the sticky area with vegetable oil and wash with soap and water.

◆ If your wooden patio furniture becomes mildewed, scrub with a solution of one cup of ammonia, one-half cup vinegar, one-fourth cup baking soda, and one gallon water. Wipe off excess with an absorbent cloth. When the furniture is completely dry, coat each piece with mildew-resistant paint (available at hardware stores).

◆ Use a baking-soda-and-water solution to wipe off vinyl seat cushions. Rinse and wipe dry.

◆ Keep baking soda handy when you grill outdoors or build a campfire. It's an instant, easy, and safe fire extinguisher in case of flare-ups and sparks. You can smother flames by tossing handfuls of baking soda at the base, then sprinkle embers with water. Don't leave the area until you test remains with your hands to make sure the fire is out.

Enriching the Soil

◆ In some parts of the country, fireplace ashes can be worked into the soil to make it more alkaline. In other parts of the country, such as South Texas, where I live, the soil is already alkaline, and ashes shouldn't be worked into it.

◆ Crushed eggshells can be added to potting or garden soil to make it more alkaline.

◆ Coffee grounds can be placed on the soil around acid-loving plants such as azaleas or roses.

◆ Save peels and other biodegradable garbage in a plastic ice-cream bucket and then add them to your compost pile so that it decomposes and can be used for fertilizer. Keep a lid on the bucket or it will draw flies and other insects.

◆ Aquarium water (fresh, not saltwater) is great free fertilizer for plants indoors or out, and old gravel from aquariums can be used in the bottom of flowerpots to aid drainage and provide a bit of fertilizer at the same time.

◆ Water houseplants or garden beds with the liquid left over from boiling vegetables.

◆ Water plants with cooled water from boiled eggs, potatoes, or vegetables and you'll feed your plants with minerals.

◆ Azaleas, gardenias, rhododendrons, and other plants that need an acidic soil will get yellow leaves in hard-water areas because the excess lime in the water prevents them from taking up iron from the soil. If you mix two tablespoons of cider vinegar to a quart of water and pour a cupful or so around the plant's "feet" every two or three weeks, their leaves will be green again.

Composting

The Environmental Protection Agency (EPA) tells us that yard wastes are relatively clean and biodegradable materials. Putting them into landfills not only takes up precious space, but the decomposition of these materials can contribute to the problems of methane gas, acidic leachate, and settling of landfills. Because the peak volumes of yard wastes are seasonal, incinerators designed to handle them are oversize and operate inefficiently. Also, the high moisture content of yard waste results in incomplete combustion and little total usable energy for power generation. Burning yard wastes contributes to air pollution from carbon dioxide and nitrogen oxide.

Because of this, some progressive cities have community compost programs where yard waste is collected separately for composting and the resulting compost material is sold for gardening. Some communities have already banned yard wastes from the regular trash pickup. But you don't have to wait for your community to get such a program. You can start your own private compost system in your yard. Here's how:

1. Find a level, well-drained, inconspicuous place in your yard. If you have a big vegetable garden, you may want to save steps and hauling efforts by building your compost pile right in the middle of it.

2. Make some sort of boundary. Most compost piles are three to four feet in diameter and get to be about four or five feet high. The compost pile needs to be about three feet across and about three feet high to be effective, and not more than five feet high because then it gets too heavy and too dense for oxygen circulation.

   A cheap and easy way to enclose the compost is to make a circle of chicken wire or wire fencing held in place with wood or metal stakes. This also allows the needed oxygen to get to the compost so that the bacteria and fungi can work to turn waste into fertilizer and mulch. You can also just make a pile and cover it with tarps to protect it from the wind. Tarps can be old blankets, sheets, bedspreads, or shower curtains staked in place or held in place with weights made from plastic gallon jugs filled with sand or water.

   Some people build two compost piles so that they always have one filled with finished compost and one in progress. However, compost can actually be used in any stage of its progress.

3. Keep the action going by feeding your compost with wilted weeds, your noncomposting neighbors' leaves and grass clippings as well as your own, orange rinds, coffee grounds, eggshells, peels and other kitchen scraps, corn husks, sawdust. Almost anything organic can go in, but avoid meat scraps and fats because they will decompose very slowly and smell bad. Pine needles and wood scraps decompose slowly and may be too acidic for some soils. Shredded newspapers used to be considered good compost material, but the most recent information from the EPA is that newsprint may contain heavy metals that can leach into your soil. The same problem exists with sewage sludge, which may contain heavy metals and pesticides.

To get information about composting materials in your area, contact your county Cooperative Extension agent or watch local gardening columns.

Since smaller pieces of material decompose faster than large, you can speed the composting process by chopping up yard waste. Put it in a pile and run a garden tiller over the pile. If you don't have a tiller, you can usually rent one from a garden center.

4. You will need to turn over the composting material every now and then to add oxygen and keep the less decomposed material at the edges blended with the more decomposed material in the center. If you turn the material over about every three days or so, it will be ready to use in about two months or longer.

5. Some people like to make "compost tea" for houseplants. Here's how: Put some compost into a bag—burlap, old pillowcase, panty hose—and hang the

bag in enough water to cover. The "brew" that results is liquid plant food.

Watering the Garden

◆ In hot climates, water lawns early in the morning or in the evening to prevent excessive water evaporation. Proper lawn watering can save 30% to 80% of normal amount of water used, and the bonus is that this saving will show up on your water bill. Watering during the day causes water evaporation up to 60% higher than watering during the evening or early-morning hours.

◆ Sprinklers that produce big drops instead of a fine mist help avoid excessive evaporation.

◆ Don't overwater lawns; excess water just runs off anyway. It's time to water when grass is a dull gray-green or if footprints remain visible.

◆ Lawns growing on sandy soil need more watering than lawns on loam or clay soils.

◆ If you keep grass about two to three inches high, roots and soil will be shaded, won't dry out so easily, and will be protected from root stress.

◆ Set a timer or alarm clock to remind you about turning off the sprinkler.

◆ Use a broom instead of a hose to "sweep" your sidewalks.

◆ If you use native plants or those that do well in your climate, you may not need to water them as often. Contact your county's Cooperative Extension agent for this information or read local newspaper gardening columns.

◆ Group together shrubs, flower beds, and other plantings that have similar water needs. Grass should be watered separately from shrubs, flower beds, and other plantings.

◆ Trees, shrubs, garden flowers, and ground covers are best watered with low-volume drip, spray, or bubbler devices.

◆ Mulching flower beds conserves moisture. Organic mulches include bark chips, woodchips, and compost in any stage of decomposition. Many people also use leaves of live oak trees, pine needles, and pine cones. Inorganic mulches include rock and gravel. Man-made mulches include plastic film and old newspapers.

Plant and Yard Pests

It's most important not to invite pests to your home. Always avoid having standing water in containers, old tires, or low areas because it provides breeding places for mosquitoes. Yards in which pets live and which are not "poop-scooped" attract flies. Litter attracts rodents. Woodpiles near the house attract termites.

Handpicking weeds from turf and pests from plants, trapping rodents and some insects, screening to keep mosquitoes out, and plugging cracks and crevices to keep roaches and other insects out are not quick methods of pest control, but they are safe for you, your pets, wildlife, and the environment.

◆ If purple martins will nest in your area, one of the best "pesticides" you can put into your garden is a purple martin birdhouse. These birds, who like apartment-style birdhouses, will eat thousands of insects daily. Plans for purple martin houses are found in craft books and magazines, and often country craft shows will have at least one display of birdhouses. Praying mantises and ladybugs are other insect-eating friends in your yard.

◆ Cardboard rolls from paper towels and toilet tissue can be poked into the ground as "collars" to protect tiny seedlings from insects and strong wind.

◆ The following concoction may discourage deer and other animals (and some insects) from eating your plants: In a blender, combine one cup water, five garlic cloves, and six large hot peppers. Blend thoroughly, then strain and pour the mixture into a spray bottle that holds two cups of water. Apply liberally whenever needed.

◆ Cats don't usually like citrus smells, so scatter lemon, grapefruit, and orange peels near plants that need protection from them.

◆ If you drizzle the surface of trash cans with bug spray, liquid soap, or ammonia animals will probably leave them alone. Inserting a trash can into the hole of an old tire will make it tipproof to curious animals.

◆ Keep your curious puppy away from houseplants by rubbing the leaves and stalks with a cotton ball saturated with hot pepper sauce.

◆ Japanese beetles are a problem in many areas. Here is a trap you can make: Open a can of fruit cocktail and put it in the sun—but out of the rain—to ferment for about a week. Place the can on a stack of bricks inside a yellow-colored pail or dishpan. Place the pail or pan about 25 feet away from the plants to be protected and fill it with water to a level that's just below the fruit cocktail can. The beetles will feast on the fruit and then drown in the water. If rain dilutes their "beetle buffet," you'll have to replace it because beetles like it potent.

◆ To get rid of red spider mites, mix four tablespoons of dishwashing liquid or one-half cake of dissolved yellow soap in one gallon of water. Spray plants weekly until mites are gone and then monthly to keep them from returning.

◆ To control spider mites on fruit trees, mix one-fourth cup buttermilk and two cups of wheat flour with two and a half gallons of water. You'll have to mix the flour and water first to get rid of lumps and then strain the mixture so it won't clog your sprayer. Also, shake the mixture well before each use. For best results, spray three times, seven days apart.

◆ Another pesticide safe for fruit trees is a mixture of garlic and mineral oil. Chop or put through a garlic press one whole garlic bulb (that's a bulb, not a bud!) and let it sit for a couple of days in a glass jar with several ounces of mineral oil. Mix a few spoonfuls with dishwashing liquid and dilute with water. Spray with a sprayer. Add a bit of hot pepper sauce to this mixture and pour it where rabbits, gophers, and woodchucks roam and they will be discouraged and stay away. The mixture also repels beetles from tomatoes, peppers, potatoes, and some other plants.

◆ Put cucumber peels on an ant route and they will go away.

◆ Treat hardshell scale on plants by mixing one-fourth teaspoon olive oil, two tablespoons baking soda, and one tablespoon mild liquid soap in two gallons of water. Spray or wipe on plants once a week for three weeks. Repeat if necessary.

◆ You can also get rid of scale by applying buttermilk or sour milk on infested areas with a cloth or paintbrush. Wait a while and then rub off dead insects and dispose of them in a sealed container to prevent any that remain alive from reinfecting your garden.

◆ Get rid of mealy bugs by wiping affected areas with cotton swabs dipped in alcohol. Spray larger plants weekly with a solution of one part alcohol to three parts water until the bugs stop hatching. Use a light touch because alcohol can burn tender foliage.

◆ If you need an insecticide for indoor plants, mix five drops of dishwashing liquid in one quart of tepid water, then spray plant leaves weekly.

◆ Nicotine kills aphids, fungus gnats, springtails, symphyllids, and some other garden pests and is an ingredient in some commercial preparations. Make your own nicotine preparation by soaking two or three cigarette or cigar butts in a can of water until you have a brown "tea." Adding dishwashing liquid to this tea makes it more potent and helps it to spread better. Use it on plants and soil but not on edible leaves, because nicotine is a toxic substance. (But you knew that, right?)

Also, do not use this on plants in the nightshade (Solanaceae) family, such as petunias, peppers, potatoes, tomatoes, and nicotiana because it can cause tobacco mosaic disease. If you still smoke, you need to wash your hands before handling the plants listed above. Nicotine on your hands can infect them with tobacco mosaic. Milk is said to destroy the tobacco mosaic virus and so a milk rinse is insurance against your spreading the disease.

◆ Fill a shallow pan with beer and leave it near garden plants overnight. Garden snails and slugs will crawl in for a sip and drown.

◆ Vinegar in a shallow pan will attract snails and slugs to plunge to their demise.

◆ You can also spray snails and slugs with a mixture of half vinegar and half water.

CAUTION: White vinegar might harm some plants. Just spray the slugs and snails, not the foliage.

◆ Salt sprinkled on snails and slugs kills them immediately. To launch a major assault on them, go out in your garden at night with a flashlight and a saltshaker.

◆ If you're too busy at night, place "cups" from orange or grapefruit halves open side down at different places in your garden and then go out in the morning to search and destroy with your saltshaker.

◆ Fleas in your house can be made to drown themselves. Place a shallow pan of sudsy water on the floor under a lamp that is the only light in the room, and leave it overnight. (More on fleas in the "Household Pests" section.)

◆ Flies in your garbage can? Wash the cans thoroughly, let them dry in the sun, then sprinkle dry laundry soap in the bottoms; it keeps flies away.

Gardening Aids

◆ Cut the handle and worn bristles from old worn-down brooms and then poke the handle end into the ground near your door so that you can wipe your garden-messed shoes on it. The long cut-off handle can be used as an extra closet rod or garden stake.

◆ Fill milk and bleach bottles that have handles with water or sand and use them to weigh down the ends of tarps or plastic used to protect tender bedding plants when frost is expected during the night.

◆ An old laundry or fruit basket will shade and protect small plants from wind if you place it over the plants upside down.

◆ Use hopelessly burned stove burner covers for pot plant saucers.

◆ Plant seedlings in cracked cups and saucers. They'll look pretty and fit on a sunny windowsill.

◆ Tie tomato plants to stakes with old panty hose or panty-hose twine. They are sturdy in the roughest weather but gentle to the stalks. (Directions for making panty-hose twine are in the "Arts and Crafts" section.)

◆ You can tie up bushes to trellises, or fences, too, and brown panty hose just blend in with the branches of bushes and shrubs.

◆ To hang up small houseplants outdoors, slip the pot into a panty-hose foot, make four cuts in the stocking from the rim of the pot to the end of the stocking, then twist each strand into a rope and tie your hanging "hose basket" to a tree branch.

◆ To prop garden tools against the wall of a garage and keep them there, make a panty-hose "rack." Insert one panty-hose leg into another so you have double strength, then thumbtack the leg strip to the wall at about four- or five-inch intervals, leaving a bit of slack in between so that you can insert the handles of shovels, rakes, brooms, and other garden tools.

◆ Make a soap-on-a-rope by inserting leftover soap bits into the toe of a panty-hose leg. Tie a knot so the pieces stay put, and then tie the other end of the leg near an outside faucet. You can wash garden hands outside and avoid messing up the bathroom or kitchen sink for whoever has that cleaning chore. Anything can be a towel—even the seat of your own jeans!

◆ Rinse out a squirt liquid detergent bottle with a push-down closure and use it to water houseplants such as African violets, which don't like to get their leaves wet. You can squirt water, with or without plant food mixed into it, under the leaves. In the yard, you can squirt water on unreachable or hanging pot plants.

◆ Many "recipes" for commercial powdered plant food make one gallon of liquid plant food. Mix in a clean plastic gallon jug and label boldly and clearly if you have to store leftover solution.

◆ Keep your greenhouse plants comfy day and night. Fill gallon plastic jugs with water, add black ink, and replace lids. The jugs will absorb heat during the day and keep your plants cool; then at night the heat absorbed by the water will keep your plants warm.

◆ If your skin is sensitive to weeds, poke your arm into a plastic dry cleaner's bag or wrap one around your arm to protect it when you're weeding in the garden.

◆ Prevent blisters and calluses from garden chores. If you have soft half-inch foam padding left from installing a carpet, wrap it around rake, shovel, and lawn mower handles, and secure it with duct tape to make padded handles.

◆ If your child no longer uses a coasting disk, you can use it to pull gardening tools around the yard; it won't damage the lawn, or the floor, either, if you use it as an indoor "wagon."

◆ Almost any bits will serve as draining stones in flower pots. Try using the top tabs from soda cans and the plastic tabs used to close bread bags, as well as broken pot pieces.

◆ Use plastic-foam packing "squiggles" and other packing bits in the bottom of pot plants to aid drainage without making the pots heavy. Plant roots will network through the squiggles.

◆ Use plastic-foam fast-food carryout containers as seedling starters and outdoor pot coasters. Break them up and use them as you would plastic foam packing squiggles.

◆ Place used coffee filters in the bottom of pots when you are planting in them. They will hold the soil but still allow drainage, and the leftover coffee grounds are good for the soil, too.

◆ Keep some plastic-foam trays handy to use as garden knee pads. They cushion and keep your knees clean. Hold them on with the tops cut off socks.

◆ You can keep your knees clean when gardening by slipping old sock tops on your legs and over your knees.

◆ Make a soaker hose from an old leaky hose. Poke more holes up and down the hose (a heated ice pick works very well) and then place the hose between vegetable rows or in garden beds. The water won't evaporate as it will with a sprinkler.

◆ If you don't feel like standing around to direct a hose toward a certain spot in your garden, bend a coat hanger into a V to hold the hose in the proper direction and then poke the straightened-out hook end of the hanger into the ground.

◆ Make a garden hose rack by hanging an old tire rim on a clothesline pole. Wrap the hose around it and no more tripping over a garden hose.

◆ Keep a garden hose neat by storing it wound up inside an old tire.

◆ Old tires can be used to build a retaining wall or for hillside steps. For steps, dig in just far enough to lay the tire flat and slightly overlapping, then fill with dirt or sand. If you make a whole hillside into "steps" with old tires, you can plant pretty native flowers in the soil, which won't run off when it rains.

◆ Old tires can be made into raised planters if you place them on the ground, one or two deep, and then fill them with soil. You can paint them or plant flowers or greenery that will drape over the edges and cover the tires.

◆ Use pieces of string as wicks for watering plants that don't like overwatering, or while you are on a trip. Poke the wick into the hole in the bottom of a clay pot and put the other end into a container of water. The plant will slurp up the water it needs when it needs it.

◆ To maintain houseplants while you are gone a few days: Place them in front of a sunny window or door under a card table. Make a terrarium by draping clear plastic, such as dry cleaner's bags, over the table sides to make an enclosure. Put another sheet of plastic, or large piece of cardboard or other thick paper padding, under the plants to protect the floor/carpet from moisture.

◆ To keep cut flowers fresher longer, pour a mixture of equal parts nondiet lemon-lime soda and warm water into the vase; it will provide the clean water, acidity, oxygen, and sugar that cut flowers like. Inexpensive generic soda is fine for this mix.

◆ Leaky vase? For a fine crack, hold the vase upside down over a light to find the leak, then patch the leak by dripping epoxy glue on it. Let it harden and it will hold water. If the vase has a larger, unsealable crack, just put a plastic bag inside as a liner. The water will keep the bag in place.

◆ Any two-quart plastic jug from milk, detergent, or fabric softener can be cleaned and used to water plants. You can mix up your plant food and save the remainder for another time. Or punch holes in the kind of bottle that has a soft plastic snap-on lid, and you have a sprinkling can.

CAUTION: Always clearly mark containers of homemade mixtures for house or garden so that they don't cause harm to people or pets.

◆ Heavy plastic gallon jugs of any color can have their tops and bottoms cut off and be cut into panels for use as row or bed markers in your garden. Be sure to use waterproof markers! You can also use plastic-foam meat trays for markers.

◆ Plastic containers of all sizes can have tops and bottoms cut off so that they serve as collars for seedlings. Cans work, too, but in very warm climates, they may absorb too much heat and burn plants.

◆ Two-liter plastic soda bottles have many indoor/outdoor garden uses:

> 1. Cut off the bottoms and use them as flowerpots. The black plastic bottoms of some bottles will come off easily if you run hot water over them; they already

have drain holes for use as flowerpots. You can punch holes along the rim with a paper punch, attach twine, and hang light-weight plants in them.

2. Cut off the tops at the edge of the dark section and use the top over newly planted vegetable or flower seedlings to protect them from insects and strong wind.

3. Cut off the tops at the edge of the black (or colored) section. Remove the inner clear plastic from the colored section and put tiny plants or seeds in the bottom, then replace the top of the bottle, and you have a small terrarium for starting seedlings or small plants for a windowsill.

4. Cut the bottle at its shoulder and use it as a vase or container for rooting clippings.

5. Line the colored bottoms with heavy aluminum foil to make unbreakable outside ashtrays. You can put sand in them if you have some. (A good tip now that so many smokers are thoughtful and step outside to "get some air.")

◆ Paint empty plastic bottles and jugs and string them together and you'll have a string of "gourds" to decorate your patio.

◆ Old carpet or carpet remnants can be cut for strips to fit the paths between garden rows. You'll be keeping the weeds from growing and keeping your shoes clean at the same time.

LIST OF RECYCLABLES INSIDE
AND OUTSIDE THE HOUSE

Aluminum pie pans and dinner trays
Ashes
Ashtrays
Bags, brown paper, insulated ice cream

Calendar pads
Cans
Cardboard boxes, tubes
Cartons, ice-cream or chips
Cereal boxes and liners
Coat hangers
Greeting cards
Carpet remnants
Coffee grounds
Elastic from men's shorts or panty hose
Fast-food containers
File folders
Filters, used coffee
Foam carpet padding
Foam ice chest
Garden hose
Giftwrap
Glass jars
Junk mail
Laundry water, used
Lint from dryer
Neckties
Newspapers
Pants or jeans, old
Panty hose
Panty-hose packaging
Paper, used computer sheets
Paper, used napkins, plates, towels, tissue tubes
Peanut-butter pail
Plates and covers from frozen dinners
Plastic—jugs, jars, pill bottles, baby-wipe containers, soda bottles, ice-cream pails, scoops, sandwich bags, squirt bottles, bags, wrap, foam meat/veggie trays, lids, 35mm film tubes, grocery bags, fast-food holders, tabs, tubs, dry cleaner/bread/news-paper/clothing/bread/veggie and diaper bags, foam packing bits, miscellaneous containers

Rubber bands
Soap, left-over
Soda-can tabs
Softener sheets, laundry
Spray containers
Tape, adding-machine
Telephone book, old
Tire rims
Tires, old
Toothpaste, spilled

Section 3
In the Workplace

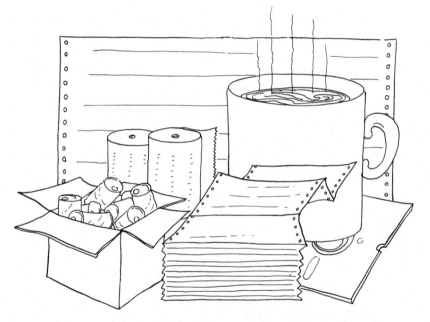

AT THE OFFICE

Often we are wasteful at work because we think a big company can afford to buy all the supplies we could ever use up. It took a wire-supply crisis several years ago and the corresponding shortage of paper clips to get some people to take paper clips off papers before tossing them into the trash.

How wasteful anyway! Now, we have to think about reusing the paper as well as the paper clips if we are to conserve our natural resources and avoid filling up our landfills with excess office trash.

To add to our new ecology awareness, we are being asked to abandon our yellow legal pads, the traditional paper used for taking notes in many offices and professions, and use white pads because yellow paper needs to be bleached, which raises the cost of recycling paper. And there's more: Our comfort zones are further invaded by those who ask us actually to write on both sides of the paper!

Most of these hints concern office work because that's my field of expertise. Most are about paper because offices are mostly about paperwork. I'm hoping that people in other workplaces will send me tips on how to conserve resources. It's good business, whatever your business, because conservation makes sense as well as cents and dollars for all of us.

♦ Conservation can be good public relations. Long computer printouts and other paper can be donated by businesses to schools to be used for painting and drawing and as scratch paper. Long computer printouts are especially good for school bulletin boards and other room decoration projects.

♦ Place a container near the soft-drink machine for aluminum cans and let a scout troop or other nonprofit organization pick up the cans for recycling fundraisers.

Or place a volunteer in charge of selling the cans and either donating the funds to charity or using them to buy coffee-break goodies for everyone to share. The amount of money may not be great in some offices, but it does keep the recycling idea in people's heads.

♦ Reduce the amount of foam coffee cups in your company's trash by bringing your own mug. The coffee tastes better, and mugs with cheery messages on them can brighten your day. (Keep some baking soda around in the coffee room to clean mugs and they won't look nasty. Fill mug with water, sprinkle in some baking soda, soak or not, and rinse.)

◆ Do you always need to have your lunch-wagon sandwich put into a bag? Sometimes you plan to eat it as you walk away from the wagon and the bag is just one more thing to toss into the trash. A wasteful habit.

◆ Do you always take a handful of individual mayos, mustards, and ketchups instead of the actual number of packets you'll use? Or a handful of napkins instead of what you need? The extras end up being just more plastic bits and paper in the trash! Multiply your handfuls by the number of people in your office and the number of working days in the year—what a waste!

◆ Use newspaper or old computer printouts for "place mats" under your lunch instead of paper towels. Newspapers absorb spills and give you something to read at the same time.

◆ Turn off the water after you wash your hands in the restroom and report leaky plumbing to the proper person instead of waiting for someone else to do it.

◆ Buy brown paper hand towels instead of white ones. The amount of waste won't change, but brown towels aren't produced with a bleaching process that requires sulphur, a chemical that contributes to water pollution.

◆ Use pens that take refills or new cartridges instead of disposable pens.

Office Paperwork

◆ When you buy a new copy machine, buy one that makes photocopies on two sides instead of just one so that you use one piece of paper instead of two.

♦ Let adding-machine tape continue to roll instead of cutting it off; reroll it around an empty tape spool, secure with a rubber band, and use the clean side for lists, phone messages, and scratch paper.

♦ A paper cutter can reduce letter- or legal-size sheets of paper that have been used on one side to smaller strips that are convenient for phone messages and scratch paper.

♦ When you use the clean sides of paper (old memos, reports) for scratch pads, stapling stacks into "pads" and/or drawing a line across the printed side keeps them from being confused with papers to file. I do this!!

♦ People who do the filing know that file folders can be used for years, but what about the others in the office? Manila folders can be reused if labels are changed on the tabs, or if you write with pencil on the tabs so that titles can be erased, or if you just use the folder inside out the second time so that the old title won't show.

♦ With continuous-roll paper used on many printers, you may waste one sheet in between documents because of the way the second document's first page gets aligned on the printer roll. One of my editors solves this problem by running off a FAX cover sheet after each document she prints. She rips off the printed document and leaves the FAX sheet in the printer roller as a spacer sheet. Any frequently used form could be printed if you don't need FAX cover sheets.

♦ If you FAX to the same people frequently, sometimes you can use the FAX cover sheet more than once, just as interoffice memo envelopes are used. Just cross off the previous FAX information and write the new information on another line. You'll also have a complete record of your FAX transmissions on one piece of paper if you need one.

♦ Some printers use either one-time film or reusable fabric ribbon. Save film for final drafts and use fabric ribbon for first drafts.

◆ Computer disks with information that is no longer needed can be erased and reused. But make sure the information isn't needed, or you might find yourself using up a lot of paper for printing and mailing out résumés in your search for a new job!

Home Offices

Home offices can usually be less formal and therefore recycle more office paper and "equipment."

◆ Express Mail letter pouches made from heavy cardboard make good file envelopes for bits and pieces such as small receipts and bills. Make an identification tab from a self-stick label folded so that about a half-inch sticks out to identify the folder.

◆ Large boxes that stationery comes in can be used as storage files. Some even hold hanging-file folders.

◆ Computer-paper boxes can also be used as storage files.

◆ Some brands of computer paper come in boxes with handles. These boxes are convenient portable files in which to keep information ready to carry to a meeting or book manuscripts to take to your publisher or agent if you are lucky enough to have either one.

◆ Children's outmoded ring binders and colored folders can hold notes and other printed information so that it's handy for reference.

◆ Unused pages from school spiral notebooks can be used. Either tear out the clean paper and leave the written material in the notebook for saving, or tear out the written material and staple it (or put it into a ring binder) to be saved.

◆ Children's unused bulletin boards and chalk boards are useful for messages and reminders in a home office.

◆ If you really can write only on one side of the paper in a secretary's notebook when you take notes, write with blue pen on one side. When you have filled all the pages, reverse the notebook and write on the other side with black pen.

◆ Cracked mugs and other containers can hold pencils on the desk.

◆ Place old and new phone books under your desk and they'll be handy as a foot stool as well as a reference.

◆ Cut a cereal box crosswise across the front to get two triangular holders for magazines and thin reference books.

◆ An old hollow door can be a desk if it's placed over two file cabinets (one on each end) or two stacks of two plastic milk carton carriers each (stacked on their sides so they are also open for storage).

◆ Don't forget the old student's bookcase made from bricks, concrete blocks, or milk crates (stacked on their sides), and boards. It helps and is economical in a home office, too.

◆ If you don't like the rustic look of brick bookends, cover them with cloth, needlework, or anything that won't be too slippery on the shelf.

◆ Instead of throwing away self-sticking name tags worn home from meetings or promotional bumper stickers you get at various events, cover your file cabinets with them. You'll have lots of memories stuck on your files instead of just more trash on the curb.

Workplaces Other Than Offices

I'm hoping people in other occupations will write me their hints for reducing trash output and conserving resources.

Wherever you work, please send hints to Heloise, P.O.

Box 795000, San Antonio, TX 78279. Or FAX them to 1-512-HELOISE.

LIST OF RECYCLABLES IN THE WORKPLACE

Adding-machine tape
Aluminum cans
Binders, ring
Bumper stickers
Colored folders
Computer-paper boxes
Computer printouts
Express Mail pouches
FAX cover sheet
File folders
Name tags
Newspaper
Paper, writing
Stationery boxes
Steno books

Section 4
Play and Entertainment

HOBBIES

Arts and Crafts

Taking things that might otherwise get discarded and turning them into useful or decorative objets d'art or, in some cases, just "objet de household" can be fun as well as environmentally conscientious. And if the project turns out to be less than decorative or in fact downright ugly, you can throw it away without any serious loss of money or self-esteem!

Sometimes art instructors in schools, daycare centers, and scout troops have uses for items that the rest of us throw away, such as cardboard rolls from paper towels and foil, baby-food jars with lids, wooden ice-cream pop sticks, yarn, string, bits of lace, magazines, egg cartons, milk jugs, empty thread spools, egg cartons, buttons, fabric remnants, old toys and kitchen items, shoestrings, sawdust, squeeze bottles, spice jars, children's clothing, towels, old toys, computer paper, shirt cardboards, and more. A simple phone call to school art departments could make your would-be trash someone else's treasure and save school tax dollars as well.

I list below a number of craft ideas sent to me by readers and given to me by friends. I'm sure there are many more and I'm hoping that you will send your ideas to me so that I can share them with others.

♦ Flattening plastic jugs or bottles for craft projects is as easy as one-two-three.

1. Cut off the tops and bottoms and then cut them lengthwise so that they will ultimately open flat.
2. Soak them in very hot water for 10 to 15 minutes.
3. Place them between paper towels or brown paper bags, to cool, weighted with a fat board, bricks, or books (protected from moisture by plastic).

After cooling, they can be marked with a pattern or have holes punched into them with a paper punch for lacing with yarn or twine, and used as desired.

♦ Faded plastic flowers can be reused for craft projects that will be spray-painted. (Wear a rubber glove so that you don't get paint on your fingers when spray-painting.)

◆ Baby-food jars can be decorated with paints that adhere to glass so that they can display or store various things such as spices, teas, earrings, fishing flies, and other small objects.

1. Baby-food jars can also be made into attractive paperweights. Children can insert colorful plastic animals and insects found in dime stores or fishing flies from sporting goods stores, then pour in varicolored sand or small gravel, fill jar to the top with water, and tighten the cap, shake a bit, and reverse, allowing the gravel to settle with the lighter plastic objects on top.
2. Fill jars with small seashells, add plain sand, screw the lid on, and reverse jar for a less colorful, more "adult"-looking paperweight. Jar lids can be painted with metal-adhering paint for a finishing touch.
3. Glue plastic ferns, flowers, critters, and pebbles on the inside of the lid with waterproof glue for a forest scene and after the glue dries, add water and white glitter for a shake-up snow scene that will amuse a sick-a-bed child for hours. An older child could do this as a keep-busy project or gift item.

◆ Paint jar tops of nicely shaped jars and use them to hold gift candy and other homemade goodies, especially at Christmas, when you can also glue greenery or ornaments, glitter, or ribbons on the jar and/or lid. You could wrap individual pieces of homemade fudge in colored or silver foil and present them in a decorated instant coffee jar for a pretty, mouth-watering gift.

◆ Empty paper-towel rolls can be covered with construction paper or colored with felt-tip markers by children and used for napkin rings at parties or just for everyday fun.

Adults who can do papier-mâché can glue at least three layers of tissue strips (about one-half- to one-inch wide by about two inches long) on one- to two-inch lengths of paper-towel or toilet-tissue rolls (overlap edges with tissue toward the inside, too, for a finished look), glue on a border of string (dipped in glue) about one-fourth inch from each edge, and then, after the glue is dry, paint them with colors to match china or linens. You can use tissue from the inside of gift boxes or tissue wrap for this project; the pieces get crumpled anyhow. Small dried flowers, beads, shells, or other decorations can also be glued on these napkin rings, which last a long time.

◆ This papier-mâché technique can also be used to cover picture frames that have seen better days. Older children can make simple papier-mâché picture frames using this technique over cardboard.

◆ Frame graduation or wedding announcements or pretty invitations and return them to senders for a sentimental gift using school or bridesmaid-dress colors for matting and/or framing. One of my favorites.

◆ Many wine and liquor bottles have beautiful shapes that can be enhanced with papier-mâché or by wrapping with twine and then finishing with paint or lacquer. Wine bottles left from special occasions can bring back memories of happy days each time you look at them.

◆ If you want to use a bottle that has a cork stuck inside, pour ammonia in the bottle, keep it in a place with good air circulation, and in about a week, the cork will disintegrate so that you can wash the insides clean.

◆ Many bottles and jugs can be hung up indoors or out with macramé holders and used as ivy planters.

◆ Need a scrapbook for newspaper and magazine clippings? Use last year's phonebook and file each article alphabetically using the guides on its pages. You don't even need to glue the articles, just file 'em!

◆ Painting small objects, such as plastic model parts, numbers to attach to your front door, or beads for craft projects? Fasten them to an inverted plastic-foam tray with toothpicks. They'll stay put while you paint and you'll have cleaner hands.

◆ Make drink coasters from plastic-foam trays by gluing on shells, sequins, buttons, lace, and other trimmings.

◆ The colored plastic clips you get on plastic bread bags can be used as mosaic "tiles" if you cut off the hole part and then trim the corners of this cut at angles to match the other corners. The finished tab has eight sides. One of my readers embedded the tabs in a cement doorstep just as one would use tiles, including making a border at the step's edge.

◆ Use the plastic tabs from bread bags as free guitar picks.

◆ Old panty-hose legs and feet can be filled with grated, scented soap, herbs, or spices, knotted, and then hung in the bathroom for an herb scent that's released when people heat the room with their baths or showers.

◆ Colorful labels from cans and bottles can be removed with a hot-water soak, dried, and glued in a collage-style on appropriate containers for canisters, wastebaskets, recipe boxes, and homemade scrapbooks. Wine-bottle labels could be glued on a scrapbook of wine information, food labels on a recipe shoe box, and so on. I have seen screens and lampshades on which wine labels have been glued, but remember, some of the labels need sealer before they are finished with varnish or shellac. Consult the folks at a craft store.

◆ Plastic plates from frozen meals can be the bases for decorative trays. Glue a small mirror in the center, frame with lace, braid, or other trim, then use as a tray for perfume bottles, cosmetics, and other small items. Or decorate them with pretty decals.

◆ Completely clear plastic lids, such as those that cover liver or deli foods can be "crystal" decorations to hang on your Christmas tree or in windows. Draw designs on the lid with

Magic Markers, punch a hole in the edge for the hanger, place the lid on a cookie sheet or foil, then put it into a 450° oven for about one minute. The lid will shrink into a tiny plastic disk. If you wish, you can press it flat with a spatula while it's still warm. Hang with yarn or clear fishing line.

◆ A half-gallon milk container becomes a bird feeder if you cut a "window" piece from the side of the carton or jug, paint the carton inside and out (optional), and put a dowel or piece of tree branch beneath the "window" to be a perch. Fill bottom with birdseed and hang by the top "roof."

◆ The tops of tin cans can be hole-punched with a nail and strung together for a windchime. Practice bending the tops to get the right tone. Use needle-nose pliers and wear thick gloves to protect your hands from cuts.

◆ The rings on the ends of paper juice cans are good for making mobiles.

◆ After removing the top of a tin can and washing the can out, you can pound nail holes in the sides in any design that you like for an outdoor candle holder. Large cans with lighted candles inside lined up along your front walk when you have a party will help guests find your house.

◆ Make "track lighting" by buying the electrical parts and using medium-sized tin cans painted black as light-bulb covers or "shades."

◆ If you have a glass cutter, you can make drinking glasses from mineral-water, wine, or beer bottles, or bowls from larger bottles. The bottoms of champagne bottles can be made into outdoor ashtrays or indoor paper-clip holders. You need to finish the edges with wet or dry extra fine sandpaper.

◆ An umbrella that has lost its fabric can be opened and hung upside down so that you can clip wet watercolor paintings or other crafts on it for drying; or more practical but less fun, hang lightweight wet laundry on its spokes. If you decorate the umbrella, you can use it to hang kitchenwares, scarfs, or necklaces for both storage and decoration.

◆ If you are lucky enough to get one, large wooden spools that are used for telephone cable make good outdoor tables. You can paint them or trim the table-top edge with ball-fringe or braid. You'll even have a hole in the center for an umbrella!

◆ Here's a library workshop tip for folks who take out several books at a time and want to tell at a glance when the books need returning: Cut strips from brown paper grocery sacks and tape the ends together to make a band that will slide onto the front cover of a library book. With a large marking pen write the words "date due" and "card holder" on the band. Write the date and name of the person who checked out the book with pencil so the book band can be erased and reused. In families, you could color-code the marking pens to tell quickly whose book it is.

◆ If you've stuck adhesive-backed plastic on shelves or other surfaces when doing crafts, you can remove it by placing a warm iron on the plastic with a protective cloth or aluminum foil in between iron and plastic; when warmed, paper should peel off.

◆ To remove labels from containers for recycling, soak in water or apply vinegar, allow to set awhile, and scrub off the label and residue. Sticky residue from some labels comes off with nail polish remover, alcohol, laundry spray, or, sometimes, hair spray.

Sewing and Needlework

Traditionally, those who sew and do needlework look upon creative use of leftover scraps as a natural extension of their craft. Needleworkers have always made afghans and other items with yarn left over from other projects. Anyone who sews keeps bits of trim and tape because "you never know when you'll need a piece of that color." Fabric scraps traditionally have been made into quilts, which are considered American folk art and are as suitable for wall hangings as they are for keeping us cozy and warm.

Another tradition—making rag rugs from remnants of bedding, clothing, and other fabrics that can't be recycled into other clothing or quilts—is being revived for the sake of art, not just ecology. Rag strips are also used to make place mats and table runners.

Rug "bees" are like quilting bees. Several people gather to cut and sew strips and then send them to local artisans for weaving. With instruction from a weaver or a book, you can make your own beautiful rag rugs.

Here are some hints for and from people who sew and do needlework:

◆ Instead of quilt batting, try using old blankets or sewn-together pieces of coating and other heavy wool.

◆ Keep sewing notions in clean, empty pill bottles. Some of the clear plastic cylinder shapes are perfect for holding your round bobbins all in a row without tangled threads.

◆ The long plastic bags from home-delivered newspapers will keep skeins of yarn for knitting or crocheting clean and untangled.

◆ Often, draperies outlast the bedding or upholstery they matched. If you sew, you can make large decorative pillowcases that save money and solve storage problems at the same time. Sew in a zipper on one end so that you can store blankets and extra bed pillows in these oversize cushions. They can be curled up on in a quiet reading corner or on the floor by folks who like to lie down in front of the TV.

◆ Bedspreads and quilts often wear out in the middle. If you cut the corners into squares and hem the edges, you'll have lap robes to give to nursing homes and hospitals, and to curl up under on cool TV nights.

◆ Empty thread spools have many uses:

1. Wrap leftover lengths of trim and bias tape on them to prevent tangles.
2. Wrap wet hair ribbons around them to dry without wrinkles.
3. They make good birthday cake candle holders, especially the gold ones.
4. Nail them to bureau drawers that have lost their drawer pulls.
5. Fasten a row of wooden spools, aligned rim to rim, inside the kitchen cabinet door and you have a concealed knife holder. The knife handles rest on the spools and the blades fit through the gaps between each pair. To attach the spools to the door, glue the base of each spool to the door and screw through the center hole. If you have extra long knives, add a second row to accommodate the longer blades. Varnish or paint according to your cabinet finish.

◆ A plastic grocery or shopping bag will hold a whole sewing project (fabric, pattern, notions) together, and those with handles can be hung on a doorknob or pegboard.

◆ Hang a handled plastic grocery bag near your sewing machine so you can toss in fabric and scraps.

◆ Duplicate patterns on brown paper sacks so that you can make adjustments without accidentally damaging the original pattern.

◆ Brown-paper-sack duplicates of craft projects such as stuffed animals and appliqués are sturdy enough to be used many times more than the original tissue patterns.

◆ Make a sewing kit for traveling by wrapping leftover bits of thread on a piece of cardboard that previously held bias tape. Drop in a plastic bag.

◆ Plastic connecting rings from beverage six-packs are dangerous for small animals if discarded because animals can get their little heads caught hopelessly in the rings. Cut the loops before discarding them or use them for crafts.

1. The rings will hold embroidery threads separately and untangled. Loop strands on inner and outer sections so that each loop holds several colors. You can store thread on the rings when the project is finished.
2. Staple or sew several together to make a beach bag for your towel and suit. It won't carry sand back to the car.
3. Hang a six-pack of loops in the corner of your bedroom or in your closet so that you can loop in its holes scarfs, hair ropes and ribbons, belts, and other things that usually get crushed in drawers.
4. Hang one section on a cup hook in your laundry room and poke into the loops the panty hose and fragile bras that can't go into the dryer.

◆ The small rings from plastic milk-jug caps can be used as a base for crocheting ring-pulls for shades, matching curtain or shade colors. Crochet and link several rings together for a trivet in a color that matches your linens or china. Or use the rings for napkin rings.

◆ The plastic clips that come on many clothes such as shirts and blouses will hold the ends of leftover trimming and bias tape on their cards.

◆ When you sew small cloth animals, stuff them with cut-up panty hose for easy washing. You can also replace the stuffing in ready-made animals and dolls with panty hose.

Knit fabric scraps, seam trimmings, thread clippings,

bits of yarn, used foam dryer softener sheets, the foam from foam-backed chair or sofa throws, nylon underwear, dryer lint, and other scraps can supplement stuffing.

◆ Make animal toys from an old fake fur coat or jacket.

◆ Make "yarn" for crocheting by cutting off the elastic of old panty hose, then cut a continuous strip one or two inches wide through the panty, spiraling down to the toe of one of the legs; repeat with the other leg, and then wind the strips into a ball. You can crochet hats and scarfs; knit or crochet granny squares for a small afghan; hook a rug; or crochet dishwashing scrubbers. Or use these strips for webbing in chairs with removable seats.

◆ Whole panty-hose legs can be made into rag-rug runners using sturdy thread as the warp (on a loom, the lengthwise threads) and the hose as the woof (crosswise threads).

◆ Insert the elastic from panty hose into sleeve cuffs and you can push them up comfortably.

◆ Wear the elastic under the belt of a sheath dress. You can make even gathers at the waist or make a blouson, using the elastic to hold the dress bodice in place, then putting the belt on over it.

◆ Slip too long for your skirt and you're in a hurry? Hike the slip up under the bust and hold it in place with panty-hose elastic.

◆ Keep your shirttail in with panty-hose elastic worn inside your skirt or pants.

◆ Make Easter scenes from small chicks or rabbits and arrange in plastic "egg" panty-hose containers for Easter decorations.

◆ Not all plastic "eggs" from panty hose need to be Easter eggs. Decorate them with Christmas themes and fill them with coins, rings, necklaces, or small toys for children's stocking stuffers. Or just decorate and hang on your "green" tree.

Rec-Tech Recyclables

The canisters from 35mm film are sturdy and seal tightly. I've listed some reuses here and more in the "Travel" section of this chapter.

♦ If you do a lot of photography and have more canisters than you can possibly reuse, contact daycare centers and nursery schools, which can use them for "auditory discrimination" games. Containers are filled with different small objects such as pennies, rice, or sand, and children shake them to guess what's inside. They are also used as musical shakers.

♦ The canisters will hold paper clips, straight pins, buttons, rubber bands, game pieces, and other small bits and pieces.

♦ Use them for a snowman's (or woman's) eyes instead of charcoal. They don't make mittens dirty!

♦ One canister will hold more than six dollars' worth of quarters. Store in your car ready for tollbooths and parking meters.

♦ If you punch a hole in the lid, then put both ends of a string through the hole and tie a large knot so that it's inside the lid, you can hang the canister around your or a schoolchild's neck to hold such things as a hiking first-aid kit, lunch money or bus fare, pills, and so forth.

♦ One canister will hold two bandages, one cotton ball, and an alcohol pad and serve as a pocket-sized first-aid kit.

♦ Film canisters can be made into children's dresser-drawer knobs.

♦ Old tape-recorder tape stretches and doesn't damage tender stems if you use it to tie up tomato, bean, and other garden or houseplants.

♦ Some spaghetti boxes are the right shape for storing slides.

♦ Cover a useless, warped, scratched record with foil or a doily and use it as a cake plate when you are donating to a bake sale or taking a cake to a friend.

GIFTWRAP AND GREETING CARDS

"Pre-owned" is a nice word for "used" in the automobile and secondhand clothing markets. Giftwrap and cards are so pretty, I think "pre-enjoyed" is an appropriate term in this section.

Pre-enjoyed Giftwrap and Greeting Cards

♦ You can reuse gift bows that have lost their stickum by pressing on a bit of double-stick carpet tape. Leave the backing on one side of the tape until you have a package to stick the bow onto.

♦ Save your family's Christmas gift tags from year to year and reuse them on family gifts. Children enjoy finding those they wrote; you can even put the year on them to see how handwriting changes throughout the years.

♦ Cut up scraps of leftover giftwrap and the uncrinkled parts of used wrap and use the pieces to wrap letters or checks before putting them into the envelope to prevent "see-through" envelopes.

♦ To smooth out or iron giftwrap for "one more use," press with a warm iron. When the giftwrap is warm, you can more easily remove tape, too. Some types of wrap can be sprayed with water from a pump-spray bottle and then ironed smooth.

♦ Iron paper bags with special designs on them, such as those from card or gift boutiques and specialty shops, for reuse as giftwrap.

♦ Wedding and baby-shower paper can make a sentimental liner for dresser drawers and closet and cupboard shelves. You'll remember the shower whenever you see them.

♦ If you use giftwrap to line drawers of children's dressers, you can use the paper to help identify contents. You can tell a child to get a shirt from the drawer with the teddy bears in it or put socks away in the drawer with the purple flowers.

♦ Patchwork patterns are popular. You can gather different scraps of leftover and used wrappings, tape them together on the wrong side to form squares, strips, rectangles, and whatnot for a patchwork wrap, which you can accent by tying it up with scraps of different colors and kinds of ribbons and lace.

♦ Make scratch pads for phone messages and notes by cutting up the uncrushed parts of used giftwrap.

♦ Leftover paper, cut into assorted lengths about one-fourth inch wide, can be curled with a scissor blade just like crinkle tie. You can stick the cluster of curled paper on with a bit of tape or tie it on with ribbon or real crinkle tie.

♦ Tie up a package with leftover yarn—one color or several colors combined. If you crochet, you can crochet leftover yarn into a thicker weight. Yarn ties are especially good for gifts that you send away, since bows get crushed in the mail.

♦ No yarn? No ribbon? Dip some string in dye made by combining one-half cup boiling water, one teaspoon vinegar, and several drops of food coloring. Hang out to dry and use to tie up packages or ponytails.

Gift Boxes

◆ To make a box that is reusable for storing small items, cover a well-cleaned one-half-gallon or one-gallon milk carton with self-adhesive paper after you have cut off the top, and fold the paper over the top edge to finish. Put two holes in the top, thread with ribbon or yarn, and make a bow. These boxes are good for food-gift goodies at Christmastime or for plant gifts. Nothing sticks to the waxy surface of milk cartons.

◆ Cover other types of boxes with adhesive-backed plastic so that they can be reused for storage. For example, cover a child's gift box of toy airplanes with adhesive-backed plastic in space designs and the child can use the box to store those toys. Cover an adult's gift box of towels with a floral pattern so it can be used in a linen closet.

◆ Paste pictures of babies from diaper boxes, magazine ads, and so forth and letters that spell out "Mommy," "Baby," or "Daddy" on a large box that's too big to wrap conventionally with paper, and the baby's outgrown clothing can be stored in it.

◆ Place two plastic-foam meat trays together, bottoms out, over a flat gift so the gift is the filling of this "sandwich," tape, and then wrap with paper. Money fits nicely!

◆ Very flat gifts, such as photos, scarfs, handkerchiefs, and such can be placed between two paper-pad cardboard backs used just like the meat trays.

◆ If you have no tissue paper to cushion a gift, use old dress patterns, or the comics from newspapers.

Making Gift Wrappings

◆ Take the sheets from your child's filled coloring book, tape them together, and use this paper to wrap gifts for relatives who will enjoy seeing the artworks. Who wouldn't!

◆ Send gift souvenirs from your travels in newspapers from the towns in which they were bought and you'll have wrap as interesting as the gifts inside.

◆ Wrap presents in the colored Sunday funnies or other colored sections of the newspaper. You could wrap a record in an ad for records and so forth. The lifestyle section of some papers will have large colored art on the front page that will wrap small gifts.

◆ Cut fabric scraps with pinking shears, using appropriate colors and prints (flowers for showers, kiddie prints for children) and then tie the package with leftover rickrack or ribbon. You can also cut out a design from a print fabric and glue it on a solid fabric for a center-box decoration.

◆ Wrap a present for a woman or girl with a pretty scarf.

◆ Wrap a kitchen shower gift with colorful all-purpose wiping cloths. They can be sewn together if one isn't big enough.

◆ Buy plain solid-colored glazed shelf paper or plain white butcher or freezer paper and decorate it with the fronts you've cut off last year's Christmas, birthday, or other occasion cards instead of ribbon. These are especially good for mailing, since there are no bows to squash.

◆ Buy heavy colored construction paper and paint on it swirls, squiggles, flowers, hearts, Christmas trees and wreaths, dancing stick people, anything you have a talent for, and you'll have really unique wrapping paper.

◆ Place the gift inside a pretty boutique or gift shop bag and tie a bow around its neck. Or punch two holes in the top, thread colored yarn through the holes, and tie a bow.

◆ In a pinch, you can have country-look giftwrap by placing the gift in a brown paper bag and tying the neck shut with a brightly colored calico ribbon and bow.

Storing Giftwrap

◆ Scraps of unused paper that are too small to wrap on the tube they came in can be rolled up and stored inside the tube.

◆ When putting away rolled giftwrap, poke the tubes into plastic ring six-pack beverage holders which will hold one large or two smaller rolls in each ring. It helps to stack all the rolls on a shelf; they won't roll around and, depending upon the space, can be stored on end, taking even less space.

◆ Roll yarn for gift wrapping into balls and store in a large glass jar so you can always see what you have. If the jar has an attractive lid or cork stopper, it's pretty enough to leave out.

◆ If you use giftwrap to line drawers, you'll always have some stashed away ready and waiting when you need to wrap a present in a hurry and have no time to shop.

MAKING CHILDREN'S TOYS

We have all seen children have more fun with the box and wrapping than with the gift itself. Play is fun when it's creative, and nothing is more creative than making your own toys, especially on a rainy day when "there's nothing to do." Parents and older children making toys together certainly counts as "quality time," and besides, it's fun.

Perhaps the best thing about homemade toys is that when a child is no longer interested in them, you can throw them away to make space for other things without feeling guilty about squandering money that might have been saved or used for necessities or fun, such as a day out with the family!

Fast-Fix Toys

You've heard of fast food? Here are some fast toys:

◆ Make a magic marking slate by stretching heavy plastic wrap across the bottom of a sturdy paper plate and taping it securely. You can use a dark crayon to write on this "slate" and a paper towel as an eraser.

◆ When children want to play "dress-up," cut holes in the bottoms of big paper (that's paper, never plastic) grocery bags for the head and holes on either side for arms and you have a costume. Let children decorate their clothes or costumes with crayons or markers.

◆ Make funny goggles to wear with the costume by cutting a pair of "holes" from plastic beverage rings. You can hold the goggles on with the elastic from a discarded pair of panty hose or a large rubber band.

◆ The small, long plastic containers in which tomatoes are sold can be converted to beds for small dolls.

◆ Tomato containers will hold tiny car collections neatly, and if you cut off the ends and turn the plastic container upside down you have a covered bridge for the little cars.

◆ A bottle cap can replace lost hubcaps on toy cars.

◆ Cut an opening in the lid of a shoebox, and then give a toddler such items as thread spools, measuring spoons, small balls, plastic toys—anything safe that can't be broken or swallowed—that the child can put into the box and dump out. Attach a piece of rope or heavy twine to the box, and the child can pull it around the house.

◆ Fill several plastic containers with different objects such as pennies, sand, rice, etc., making matching pairs in shape and contents, and then securely glue lids on the containers. Let preschool children try to match the sounds for a parent-child homemade sound-identification game. The containers can be used for musical shakers when the game is no longer interesting to the child.

◆ Make baby rattles (especially for use at grandparents' house) by washing out plastic containers from shampoo, conditioner, or lotion and even some larger ones from fabric softener. Fill with pebbles or bells, replace lids, and glue or otherwise tightly seal them.

◆ Similarly sized plastic vases or vase-shaped jugs can be lined up for a homemade rainy-day bowling game. Use a foam-rubber or tennis ball as a bowling ball; both are safe in the house if they are rolled.

◆ Older children can use plastic-foam meat trays to cut out parts for making airplanes. They are fairly safe for indoor flying and a lot cheaper than balsa-wood kits.

◆ An upside-down box serves as a toddler table/desk, to be either stood beside or sat at, if the box is strong enough to have a knee hole cut into it.

◆ Toddlers like to pull "trains" made by tying together boxes, or a variety of items such as a paper-towel tube, large thread spools, paper cups, and measuring cups and spoons tied so that they can be dragged around the house.

◆ Make an instant toddler train by knotting small plastic toys and other light, safe objects in a panty-hose leg; let the toddler drag it around the house.

◆ Sometimes little hands can't grasp the strings of homemade or store-bought pull toys. Take a plastic lid such as a coffee can lid and cut out the center with scissors, leaving a ring about three-eighths of an inch thick. Tie this ring to the string so that the child can find and pick up the string.

◆ A large carton with its bottom and top lids folded in for added support can be a toddler's tunnel o' fun. Older children can decorate cartons with crayons, felt-tip markers, paints, or pasted-on construction paper and magazine pictures.

♦ Blocks exercise the imagination of children of almost any age. They can be made from well-sanded scrap pieces of lumber or from different sizes of milk cartons or other boxes that have been taped shut, such as brightly colored rice, cereal, and other food boxes. Diaper boxes make good giant building blocks for forts and playhouse walls. Use as is, or cover with adhesive-backed plastic. Clean plastic jars with lids screwed on tightly can be castle turrets and towers for young architects, as can oatmeal or salt boxes.

♦ Some people find that the stiff cardboard backings for instant pictures make the pictures too thick for plastic albums with individual photo pocket pages, and so they put the prints right into the pockets without the backings. Since the backings are self-adhesive, you or older children can stick cut-out magazine pictures on the backings to make durable picture "flash cards" for young children.

♦ Play zoo. Invert plastic strawberry baskets over small plastic animals for cages.

♦ Plastic bottles, containers, and lids can be cut up and the pieces glued mosaic style on other containers for rainy-day artworks.

♦ A clean plastic milk jug with a handle can be a megaphone if you cut off the bottom and a bit of the top—enough for a junior cheerleader or would-be referee to shout through.

♦ Aluminum pieces such as disposable pie tins can be "sculpted" and bent or shaped onto bottles and other containers to make rainy-day art. Older children who won't hurt themselves dealing with sharp edges can cut up such disposables and glue them on containers or into free-form artworks. Use glue appropriate to the surfaces; read labels.

◆ An old plastic window shade that can't be attached to its roller, a plastic tablecloth, or shower curtain can save carpets when children snack or use their crayons, clay, and other messy playthings.

◆ A squirt gun made from well-cleaned dishwashing liquid bottles, the kind with squirt tops, holds more water and shoots much farther than any store-bought squirt gun. Better have the kids do this in swimsuits!

◆ If you decorate an empty oatmeal box, a child can be a drummer by beating on it with spoons or other drumsticks without giving you a headache.

◆ Inflatable plastic toys need not be discarded if they get a pinhole leak. A spot or two of clear fingernail polish will usually mend them.

Fun Projects

These can be made by parents for younger children or made as a parent-child project with older children. The project can be as simple and undecorated or as complicated and nearly store-bought as you wish. As with other toy crafts and parent-child affairs, however, don't make this project so complicated that it ceases to be fun, or the toy so elaborate that you won't let the child play with it, lest it be broken.

◆ Make a dollhouse from cardboard cartons.
Use a cardboard carton that has dividers (liquor, glassware) that can be taped in place for a second floor, or tape together several same-size boxes side-to-side, so that each forms a room.

1. Use cardboard to make furniture, too. It won't be as gorgeous as store-bought but it will be original and lots of fun.

2. Fabric and ribbon scraps can be glued on the house for drapes and on furniture for upholstery.
3. Magazine pictures of windows, rugs, plumbing fixtures, and some furniture can be cut out and glued in place on walls and floors.
4. Make mirrors for the walls of a child's dollhouse with shiny-side-out scraps of aluminum foil.
5. Cut out people and pets from magazines to live in the house. Glue pictures on cardboard and glue an "L" stand on the back so the figures can stand up.

♦ Make a shoe-box train. Paint and decorate shoe boxes according to the type of car you want. Boxes without lids are freight cars that hold toy soldiers, animals, blocks, and other cargo for transport.

1. A thread spool or jar lid can be the front of a locomotive, and spools can also be glued on top to make steam or smoke stacks.
2. For a passenger car, make windows by cutting out little squares on the sides and taping yellow cellophane on the inside. You can put a skylight in the roof of the car, too. Put a flashlight inside for best effect. Cut person profiles to glue inside the windows if you wish.
3. Connect the cars with twine, ribbon, or rope, by poking the twine end through the end of the shoe box and tying it around a frozen pop stick or other brace. If you only plan light cargo, a big knot inside or stapling a ribbon from box to box may be sufficient.

CAUTION: Don't use staples for toys for very small children, who might put them in their mouths if they come loose.

4. If you are really ambitious, you can make wheels from spools, jar lids, and other round things.

◆ Older children who have store-bought model trains often like to make villages. Small spice cans and boxes can be painted or covered with brick or wood-grain adhesive-backed plastic, to make buildings. Remains of silk or plastic greenery can be turned into shrubbery. Fencing can be made by cutting up plastic tomato containers.

◆ Make a toy kitchen from large cardboard boxes painted with appliance colors to match the family's real kitchen.

1. After the paint is dry, you can use black electrical tape to make fake knobs and other hardware on the refrigerator and stove (or attach old thread spools or parts of 35mm film canisters) for stove knobs.
2. Stove burners can be made from circles cut from aluminum pie tins.
3. For the sink, cut a square in the top of the box and put a small basin (or other box) into it. Cut the hole so the lip of a plastic basin will keep it from falling through.

◆ Make a hobby horse from old socks and a yardstick or broom handle.

1. Take a big sock for the head, using the toe for the nose and the heel for the top of the head.
2. Sew or glue on fringed fabric scraps or yarn strands for the mane and buttons for the eyes, and embroider or draw on a mouth.
3. Stuff the head with other old socks or some of the materials suggested for stuffing animals in the sewing section of this chapter.
4. Insert a stick into the opening of the sock and tie a string around it so it will stay put. If you feel like it, attach a strip of fabric, twill tape, or twine reins to the horse's neck.

Toy Storage

♦ A large cardboard box can be covered with cloth, wallpaper, or adhesive-backed plastic and then used as a toy box. Toddlers will also like to sit in the box, crawl into it, and push it around the house.

♦ Empty disposable-diaper boxes can be made into toy boxes. The handle on top makes it easy to drag, and the box can be used as is or covered with adhesive-backed plastic or old wallpaper.

♦ A well cleaned and aired-out diaper pail can become a holder of small toys after a toddler is out of diapers.

♦ A sturdy plastic bag that has pinhole leaks can hold game pieces, toy soldiers, and other bits in a child's toy box.

♦ For a neat playroom, gallon milk jugs with the tops cut off at an angle so that the handles are still intact can hold small toys and then be hung on hooks by the handles.

♦ Small toys and game pieces can be kept in coffee or other cans with plastic lids. Have the children draw or paste a picture on top to identify the contents.

♦ Adhesive bandages come in metal containers that hold crayons perfectly.

♦ Cleaned-out round ice-cream cartons have "windows" in the top so a child can see which little toys are inside.

♦ Old pocketbooks can be kiddie briefcases for play; they can be hung over the front seat's headrest for use in the car.

♦ An outgrown plastic infant bathtub is a good portable toy box. It slides on the floor from one toy pile to another for easy cleanup.

♦ A hard plastic wading pool can hold toys out of sight if you hide it under the bed.

PET STUFF

◆ A broken badminton racket can be a quick cat litter pooper-scooper.

◆ Put old newspapers under cat litter for easy litter dumping.

◆ If your cat likes to kick soiled litter all over the place, protect the wall by banking several thicknesses of newspaper or a brown paper bag against the wall next to the litterbox; secure it with masking tape. You can do this also in pet feeding corners, especially if you have a dog or cat that laps up food too enthusiastically. Plastic wrap works too!

◆ Cut used paper plates in half or use them whole as scoopers when your puppy has an accident or you must "pooper-scoop" cat litter.

◆ Use the comics or other decorative sections of the newspaper for pet feeding "place mats." One of my editors has a very lazy dog, so she always uses the "Help Wanted" classified section to inspire him to get out and earn his keep—to no avail.

◆ If you walk your dog in a park or other public area, especially in warmer weather, take along in your backpack the bottom of a two-gallon jug cut so that it has at least four-inch high sides, and you'll be able to give your dog a drink when you stop at water fountains to water yourself.

◆ You can make disposable scoops from plastic jugs—handy if you are a dog owner who lives in a city with "pooper-scooper" laws. (See the "Recycling Glass and Plastic Containers" section of this book.)

◆ Old panty-hose legs—three strands of three legs each—can be braided for a doggie tug-of-war toy.

◆ If you need an emergency pet leash, cut a slit in the toe of a panty-hose leg, then slip the toe under the pet's collar and pull the whole stocking through the slit for a sturdy loop. Knot the other end of the leg into a looped handle or just make a knot to hang on to.

♦ A blue-jean leg is a sturdy tug-of-war toy. You can even write "Tiger's Rag" on it so that nobody throws it out, thinking it's just an ordinary rag.

♦ If the kennel or vet allows it, you can send a used family-handled jeans leg with your dog when it's boarded or goes to the vet for surgery, so that your pet will have the scent of home and won't be as lonely. It doesn't matter if the jeans leg gets lost.

♦ Old panty-hose "eggs" can be filled with a few pebbles or bells, sealed shut with tape, and used by a kitten as a batting toy.

♦ You can also hook a fishing float to one end of a piece of twine and tie the other end to a doorknob for a cat toy.

TRAVEL

Packing

♦ Canisters from 35mm film hold paper clips, soap powder, talcum powder, safety pins, bobby pins, earrings, several sample lipsticks, and lots of other small items when you travel.

♦ For a traveling toothbrush holder, cut a hole in the center of a 35mm film canister lid that allows insertion of your toothbrush handle, then put your toothbrush into the round cylinder and snap on the lid.

♦ Put small sample lipsticks in film canisters for travel.

♦ Drawstring hotel plastic laundry bags make good litter bags. They also help organize your packing: You can put a day's outfit in one for a child, protect sweaters from snags, keep all of your underwear in one place, and so forth. They can even be used for dirty laundry as intended!

◆ Place underwear or panty hose inside a panty-hose leg and use the leg to pad garment folds in the suitcase so they won't become creases.

◆ Use old men's socks to cover shoes.

◆ Tuck in a terry-cloth "footie" so that you always have a washcloth.

◆ Pack a silk flower in a margarine or cottage cheese tub to keep it from being crushed.

Car Travel

◆ Hang handled plastic supermarket bags on window levers or the car radio station selector knob so it's handy for litter.

◆ Wash thoroughly and rinse well the plastic squeeze bottle (with snap cap) from jelly or ice-cream topping, and you have a nonspill juice or water bottle for the car, especially handy when you're traveling with children. Those who can't drink from the push-top spout can unscrew the lid and insert a straw. It's still neater than an open cup.

◆ Hang old pocketbooks from the front-seat headrests and you have good holders for books, crayons, and toys in the car. The bonus is that the crayons won't get left on the car seat or in the back window to melt in the sun.

Camping

Here are some free packaging items you can use when you're out in the wild:

◆ Serve food on clean plastic-foam meat and vegetable trays, frozen-dinner dishes, aluminum-foil pie pans, and similar items—but don't leave them behind to spoil nature for others.

♦ Used disposable plates of all kinds—paper, plastic, foil—can be kept to collect peelings and other bits of trash when you camp or picnic (in the kitchen, too) so that they get used one more time.

♦ The bottoms of clean plastic milk and soda bottles make good bowls at the campsite.

♦ Some clean plastic food product jugs make good lightweight water canteens.

♦ To make ice for your cooler, freeze water in quart or gallon jugs; you can drink this water as it thaws.

♦ Use the plastic sheet that comes in bacon packages as a mini cutting board and surface for forming hamburger patties for the grill.

♦ Institutional-size gallon vegetable and fruit cans can be used to boil water or cook corn on the cob, and if you punch a hole on each side and make a carrying handle from an old wire coat hanger, you can carry water in this makeshift bucket. If you never buy anything in cans of that size, ask for them at a school cafeteria or a restaurant.

♦ If you put your paper napkins in a coffee can they won't blow away. If it's very windy, put a stone inside the can.

♦ Save partly used soap bars, toothpaste tubes, and deodorant containers throughout the year so that when you take a family vacation you can make a toiletries kit for each member of the family. Such leftovers take up little space, are light weight, and don't put such a big dent in your vacation budget as buying them for everyone at the same time.

♦ For camping, make a toiletries box to take to the camp showers by covering a cardboard box inside and out with adhesive-backed plastic, making each box just big enough to hold all the toiletries. You can cut finger holes in the ends for easier gripping. You can make one family box, a men's and ladies' box, or a box for each member—whatever saves confusion.

◆ Cut the tops off plastic toothpaste tubes and wash the tubes and use them as knife or scissor sheaths. (Did you ever try cutting the bottom off a toothpaste tube, washing it out well, and using it as a decorator frosting applicator?)

◆ Tie leftover bits of soap in the toe of a panty-hose leg, and you can have a "soap-on-a-rope" to tie to a tree limb or any other convenient place.

◆ If you poke a small hole in the bottom of a clean plastic gallon milk jug, and plug it with a small cork or stick, you can hang the jug from a tree limb for running hand-washing water. (Hang your soap-on-a-rope beside it.)

◆ Old panty-hose legs will hold children's rock and seashell collections, too.

◆ Old panty hose tied together can be a strong rope for tying bundles of anything at the campsite, including sleeping-bag rolls.

◆ If you are using a card- or similar table at the campsite, put each table leg in a clean tunafish can filled with water, and the ants will have a detour en route to your picnic.

◆ Hang an opaque shower curtain from an old hula hoop, which you can hang in a tree, and you'll have a private dressing room at the campsite, or, if water is available, a shower.

Fishing

◆ Plastic-foam meat and vegetable trays can hold edible parts when you fillet fish at the pier or campsite.

◆ Hook fishing lures on plastic-foam trays or on individual foam packing "squiggles" for finger-safe storage in a tackle box.

◆ Make a fishnet by bending a coat hanger into a circle as large as the mouth of a mesh onion bag. Stitch the bag to the coat hanger and twist the hook-part of the hanger on a dowel or broomstick for extra length on the handle.

◆ Plastic milk jugs become buoys for fishing if you screw the caps on tightly and paint jugs a bright color.

◆ Did you ever lose your catch because the stringer got loose? Attach a plastic-jug buoy to the stringer so you can check with a glance whether it's still attached to your boat.

◆ Fill a plastic jug or squirt bottle with water and keep it handy near the fish-scaling area to rinse off fish scales.

◆ An empty plastic jug with a handle can be a good boat bailer. Make a scoop by screwing the cap on tightly and then cutting off the bottom of the jug. You'll have a square bailing scoop with a handle that goes into the boat's corners.

◆ Fill large jugs with sand or water to hold down tarps that cover boats or anything at the campsite.

◆ A coffee can with a lid will store your camera and keep it dry on the boat.

◆ You can scrub the bottom of your boat with a wadded-up plastic-mesh onion bag or old panty hose. If you do it at the lake, all you have to do is rinse the boat off with a hose when you get home. (Don't forget to have the boat over your lawn so the water will go to the grass instead of down the gutter.)

PLAY AND ENTERTAINMENT RECYCLABLES

Aluminum foil
Aluminum-foil pie pans

Bags—gift shop, brown paper, newspaper, mesh onion, zip-lock plastic
Beverage rings, six-pack
Blankets
Blue-jean leg
Bottles and caps
Bows, giftwrap
Boxes—Band-Aid, food, oatmeal, salt, shoe, spice, cardboard, divided cardboard cartons, milk carton, pill
Broom handle
Buttons
Cans—tin-can tops, coffee, juice, tunafish, spice, gallon food
Cardboard backs from paper pads
Cardboard bias-tape holder
Cards, greeting or gift
Coat
Coat hanger
Coat or jacket, fake fur
Coloring book
Containers—tomato, toothpaste tubes, deodorant, ice cream
Diaper pail
Drapes
Fabric scraps
Fabric seam trimmings
Film canisters
Foam softener sheets
Food jars
Glass bottles and jars
Hula hoop
Jars, baby-food
Labels, can and bottle
Lids, jar
Lint from dryer
Lumber, scrap pieces
Magazines
Newspapers

Panty hose
Panty hose "eggs"
Paper bags, specialty
Paper—cups, butcher, freezer, giftwrap, shelf, juice can ring, plates (used), towels, towel tubes
Patterns, old dress
Phone book, old
Photos, self-adhesive backings
Plastic bread-bag clips
Plastic clips from shirts
Plastic containers—handled grocery bags, grocery or shopping bags, jugs, bottles, jars, flowers, milk/soda bottles, rings from milk-jug caps, squeeze bottle, squirt bottle, strawberry baskets, shampoo/lotion containers, tomato containers, margarine or cottage cheese tubs, vases, hotel laundry bags, lids, shower curtain, tablecloth, frozen-food plates, sheets from bacon packages, window shade, wrap, foam meat or veggie trays
Plates, disposable
Pocketbooks
Racket, badminton
Records
Ribbon, leftover
Rickrack, leftover
Soap, leftover bits
Socks
Spool, large wooden cable
Spools, empty thread
Tape, old recorder
Thread, leftover
Thread clippings
Umbrella, broken
Underwear, nylon
Yardstick
Yarn, leftover

The Final Word

HOW YOU CAN HELP HEAL THE EARTH

Jeremy Rifkin, president of the Greenhouse Crisis Foundation, paints a sobering picture in his introduction to *The Greenhouse Crisis: 101 Ways to Save the Earth*, the foundation's citizens' guide.

Imagine it's the year 2035.

In an effort to hold back rising seawater, massive dikes have been built around New Orleans, New York and Miami. Phoenix is baking in its third week of temperatures over 115 degrees. Decades of drought have laid waste to the once fertile Midwest farm belt. Hurricanes batter the Gulf Coast and forest fires continue to blacken thousands of acres across the country.

During the torrid summer months large sections of the Mississippi turn into giant mudflats, closing the river to commercial traffic. In other parts of the globe, millions perish in the wake of prolonged droughts and devastating flood.

As the earth's ozone layer continues to thin, all living creatures are exposed to increasingly hazardous levels of ultraviolet radiation, causing an epidemic of skin cancer deaths. Radiation is destroying plant life and compromising the immune systems of human beings as well as the rest of the animal kingdom. In addition, acid rain has stripped the earth of a third of its remaining forests, while pollution has left many of the world's lakes and ponds virtually lifeless.

But these horrors are not inevitable. Governments, corporations, and individuals can start today to reverse the environmental damage we have already done. Each of us can help heal the earth!

Here are just a few of the Greenhouse Crisis Foundation suggestions on how each person can help. I hope you will use the following as a checklist.

Hugs for your efforts in working toward a healthy planet.

HEALTHY-PLANET CHECKLIST

◆ I've arranged for an energy audit and have fully insulated my home.

◆ I adjust my thermostat to save energy.

◆ I keep unwanted heat or cold out with curtains.

◆ I use lower-wattage bulbs and energy-efficient fluorescent bulbs.

◆ I check the energy efficiency of all appliances before I buy one.

◆ I turn off lights when I leave rooms.

◆ I carpool to work and elsewhere.

◆ I use public transportation, bike, and walk instead of driving whenever I can.

◆ I keep my car tuned up and drive at moderate speeds.

◆ I've planted trees in my yard and help my neighbors to do the same.

◆ I have a vegetable garden.

◆ I don't use plastic bags for shopping anymore.

◆ I recycle newspaper, paper, glass, and aluminum.

◆ I'm involved with environmental groups and try to learn as much as I can about saving our planet's health.

◆ I encourage my local, state, and federal officials to pass environment-saving legislation and cooperate with environmental programs in my city.

To obtain *The Greenhouse Crisis: 101 Ways to Save the Earth,* write: The Greenhouse Crisis Foundation, 1130 Seventeenth Street, NW, Suite #630, Washington, DC 20036. The cost is $5.00.

Index